ENCOUNTER
SERIES

Unsecular America

Essays by

Paul Johnson

Everett Carll Ladd

George M. Marsden

and

Richard John Neuhaus

Edited and with a foreword by

Richard John Neuhaus

WILLIAM B. EERDMANS PUBLISHING CO.
GRAND RAPIDS, MICHIGAN

BL
2525
.U57
1986

Published by Wm. B. Eerdmans Publishing Co.
in cooperation with
The Rockford Institute Center on Religion & Society

Copyright © 1986 by Wm. B. Eerdmans Publishing Co.
255 Jefferson Ave. S.E., Grand Rapids, Mich. 49503

Library of Congress Cataloging-in-Publication Data

Unsecular America.

(Encounter series ; 2)
"The essays and the discussion come out of a
conference sponsored by the Rockford Institute Center
on Religion and Society ... in New York City in
January of 1985."—Fwd.
1. United States—Religion—1960-   —Congresses.
I. Johnson, Paul, 1928-   . II. Neuhaus, Richard John.
III. Series: Encounter series (Grand Rapids, Mich.) ; 2.
BL2525.U57   1986   200'.973   86-4261
ISBN 0-8028-0202-8

Contents

083835

Foreword

Flying in the face of the facts, the conventional wisdom has until very recently been that America is or is rapidly becoming a secular society. That conventional wisdom has been repeated again and again in the communications media, high school and college textbooks, and in so many other respectable forums that many no longer think to question it. In this volume Everett Ladd of The Roper Center brings together the findings of survey research about secularity and religion in American life. The several papers in this volume and the report on the conversation that followed their presentation leave no doubt that there are many questions yet to be answered: questions about definitions of religion, about the "depth" and "authenticity" of American religiousness, about the connection between personal faith and public behavior, and so forth. The evidence presented in this book makes at least one point clear, however: Americans are as peculiarly religious as they have been thought to be in the past, and probably even more so.

That conclusion inevitably raises a series of perhaps more interesting questions, however. The famed British historian Paul Johnson addresses the question of how Americans came to be the kind of religious people they are. His essay "The Almost Chosen People" also served as the first annual Erasmus Lecture in New York City and has already stirred considerable interest. George Marsden of Calvin College examines the ways in which American religionists have viewed the "threat" of secularism, and he proposes some provocative revisions of the ways in which secularism and secularists are currently discussed. In my own essay, I attempt to relate this entire discussion to the question of whether religion might now begin to play a livelier part in renewing the American democratic experiment. As the reader will discover, the authors are skeptical, but hopefully so.

In addition to the four main essays, this book contains extensive data compiled by Everett Ladd and his colleagues as documentation for the argument he makes. And there is the "Story of an Encounter," which gives both the flavor and much of the substance of what twenty-seven scholars had to say in the discussion of the data and arguments offered.

The essays and the discussion come out of a conference sponsored by the Rockford Institute Center on Religion and Society at the Princeton Club in New York City in January of 1985. As director of the Center, I am greatly indebted to Peter Berger, our senior consultant, for his help in the planning and execution of the conference, and to my colleagues John Howard and Allan Carlson of the Rockford Institute for their support and counsel. I am most especially indebted to my associate Paul Stallsworth for seeing the conference through from concept to catering. He is also responsible for shaping the report on the discussion. Finally, my thanks, as usual, to Cynthia Littlejohn for her invaluable help as secretary of the Center.

Richard John Neuhaus

THE ROCKFORD INSTITUTE
CENTER ON RELIGION & SOCIETY
NEW YORK, NEW YORK

The Almost-Chosen People: Why America Is Different

Paul Johnson

When Abraham Lincoln called Americans "the almost-chosen people," he used an apt phrase, as valid now as when he coined it 120 years ago. It perfectly expresses the close but at the same time slightly uneasy relationship between the American republic and the religious spirit. That the Americans are exceptional in their attitude to religion is obvious to all, and never more so than today. But visitors from old Europe, such as Aleksandr Solzhenitsyn and Pope John Paul II, are struck by the way in which high church attendance and an often blatant religiosity coexist with the passionate pursuit of materialism. They are inclined to agree with Cotton Mather, who made the point as long ago as 1702 while documenting what he termed "Christ's great deeds in America" that "*religion* brought forth prosperity, and the *daughter* destroyed the *mother*. . . . There is danger lest the *enchantments* of this world make them forget *their errand into the wilderness*."

The notion of a chosen but flawed people is directly related to America's historical origins, for the first settlers were undoubtedly animated by a sense of divine mission. The work most widely read among them, after the Bible, was Foxe's *Book of Martyrs*, which vigorously expressed the dynamic myth that the English were the Elect Nation. In the sixteenth and seventeenth centuries, most English people believed that their country had received Christianity direct from Christ's disciple Joseph of Arimathea, that the Emperor Constantine was British (his mother

Helena being daughter of the British King Coilus), and that he had Christianized the whole civilized world, as Foxe put it, "by the help of the British army."

The myth was held most tenaciously among the Protestant sectarians, especially the colonists. The explorer and navigator John Davis stated, "There is no doubt but that we of England are this saved people, by the eternal and infallible presence of the Lord predestined to be sent unto these Gentiles in the sea, to those Isles and famous Kingdoms, there to preach the peace of the Lord." The creation of the Virginia colony was to be the greatest and as it turned out the only realized experiment in post-European Christianity. In a sermon to the Virginia Company in 1622, the poet John Donne, Dean of St. Paul's, told the subscribers, "Act over the Acts of the Apostles; be you a Light to the Gentiles, that sit in darkness. God taught us to make ships, not to transport ourselves, but to transport Him. You shall have made this island, which is but the suburbs of the old world, a bridge, a gallery to the new; to join all to that world that shall never grow old, the kingdom of heaven." Governor Winthrop, sailing the Atlantic on the *Arabella*, wrote, "We shall be as a city upon a hill, the eyes of all people are upon us."

It was inevitable that such elect nation-builders should place their government in a religious frame. So in a sense did all Christian nations. But whereas in the old world state authority drew its divine sanction from traditional sacral kingship, in America it took the form of conscious dedication by democratic assemblies expressed in formal documents. Those sailing on the *Mayflower* in 1620 "for the Glory of God and the advancement of the Christian faith" stated their desire "solemnly and mutually in the presence of God" to "convenant and combine ourselves together in a civill body politic."

No one who studies the key constitutional documents in American history can doubt for a moment the central and organic part played by religion in the origins and development of American republican government. The Fundamental Orders of Connecticut (1639)—the first written constitution in the modern sense of the term drawn up by popular convention and the first to embody the democratic idea—states in its prolegomena that the state owes its origin to "the wise disposition of the divine providence" and that "the word of God" requires "an orderly and decent Government established according to God" to "maintain and preserve the liberty and purity of the Gospel." Where specific provision was not laid down, magistrates were to administer justice "according to the rule of the word of God," and both governor and magistrates swore to act "according to the rule of God's word." The same principle, that the Bible was to supply any defect or omission in the written law, was articulated in the first New England law-code, the Massachusetts Body of Liberties of 1641, which was based on what is termed "humanity, civility and Christianity." It did not seem possible to these founders to distinguish between government on the one hand and religion (by which they generally meant Protestant Christianity) on the other. As William Penn put it in his *Preface to the Frame of Government of Pennsylvania* (1682), "Government seems to me a part of religion itself, a thing sacred in its institution and end . . . an emanation of the same divine power that is both author and object of pure religion."

The danger was that such quasi-religious societies would become total societies on the medieval Christian model, tolerating no dissent from established creeds and exercising the right to persecute on St. Augustine's principle of "compel them to come in." But they did not do so for two reasons. In the first place, even the churches were run by laypeople, not by the clergy. So they stressed morals and behavior rather than theology and doctrine. They moved away from the Augustinian tradition of close and detailed definition of dogma and toward the alternative proposed by Erasmus, that religion should define as little as possible and concentrate on propagating the spirit of Christian fellowship.

Since religious establishments were popular rather than hieratic, a distinctive American religious tradition began to emerge. There was never any sense of division in law between laity and clergy, between those with spiritual privileges and those without—no jealous confrontation between a secular and an ecclesiastical world. America was born Protestant and did not have to become so through revolt and struggle. It was not built on the remains of a Catholic Church or an establishment; it had no clericalism or anticlericalism. In all these respects it differed profoundly from the old world, which had been shaped by Augustinian principles and violent reaction to them. The word *secular* never had the same significance in America as in Europe because the word *clerical* had never conveyed an image of intolerance and privilege. America had a traditionless tradition, making a fresh start with a set of Protestant assumptions, taken for granted, self-evident, as the basis for a common national creed.

In any case, in a frontier society it was impossible to preserve sectarian discipline and uniformity: dissenters simply moved on. Roger Williams broke away from strict New England Calvinism to found Providence, Rhode Island, which he called "a shelter for persons distressed for conscience." His constitution (1644) defined "the form of government established in Providence Plantations as DEMOCRATICAL, that is to say a government held by the free and voluntary consent of all, or the greater part, of the free inhabitants." This was the first commonwealth in modern history to make religious freedom, as opposed to an element of toleration, the principle of its existence and a reason for separating church and state. As its charter (1663) puts it, "No person within the said colony, at any time hereafter, shall be in any wise molested, punished, disquieted or called in question, for any differences in opinion in matters of religion, and who do not actually disturb the civil peace of our said colony; but that all . . . may from time to time, and at all times hereafter, freely and fully have and enjoy his and their own judgments and consciences, in matters of religious concernments."

It is important to grasp that American society embraced the principles of voluntarism and tolerance in faith in a spirit not of secularism but of piety. Almost unconsciously the consensus grew that voluntary adherence to one faith, and tolerance of all others, was the foundation of true religion. In this respect English and American society bifurcated as early as the 1650s. While England was debating whether to have a Presbyterian or a Congregationalist settlement, and then in practice getting an Anglican one, the former governor of Massachusetts, Sir Henry Vane, was expounding the principles of civil and religious liberty (1656), arguing that they were inseparable and that freedom of religious belief was essential to the maintenance of a Christian society: "By virtue then of this supreme law, sealed and confirmed in the blood of Christ unto all men . . . all magistrates are to fear and forebear intermeddling with giving rule or imposing in those matters." This document, and the sentiments it articulated, were more instrumental in determining the spirit of the American Constitution in religious matters than were the writings of the Enlightenment.

It is probably true that the American Revolution was in essence the political and military expression of a religious movement. Certainly those who inspired it and carried it through believed they were doing God's will. Its emotional dynamic was the Great Awakening, which began in the 1730s. The man who first preached it, Jonathan Edwards, believed strongly that there was no real difference between a political and a religious emotion, both of which were God-directed. The right kind of politics were to his way of thinking no more than realized eschatology. He said he saw no reason why God should not "establish a constitution" whereby human creatures should cooperate with him and all might know that the hour was coming when God "shall take the kingdom"; he looked for "the dawn of that glorious day."

Edwards saw religion as the essential unifying force in American society, and that force was personified in his evangelical successor George Whitefield. Until this time America was a series of very different states with little contact with each other, often with stronger links to Europe than to their neighbors. Religious evangelism was the first continental phenomenon, transcending differences between the colonies, dissolving state boundaries, and introducing truly national figures. Whitefield was the first American celebrity, as well known in New Hampshire as in Georgia. His form of religious ecumenicalism preceded and shaped political unity. It popularized the real ethic of the American Revolution, which was not so much political as social and religious—the beliefs and standards and attitudes that the great majority of the American people had in common. It was a Christian and to a great extent a Protestant ethic, infinitely more important than the purely dogmatic variations of the sects.

It is worth remembering that the key state in the formation of the union—Pennsylvania—was the most diverse in religion. It was a Presbyterian stronghold, the headquarters of the Baptists, a state in which Anglicanism was strong and Catholicism flourished, home to a variety of Mennonites, Moravians, and German pietists, as well as Quakers and other sects. The Declaration of Independence and the Constitution were thus framed in an appropriate setting (it was also the center of America's economic communications). The institution of religious freedom and of a state that did not distinguish between faiths was the work not so much of millenarian sects revolting against magisterial churchmen as of the denominational leaders and statesmen themselves, who saw that pluralism was the only form consonant with the ideals and necessities of the country.

Even those most strongly influenced by the secular spirit of the Enlightenment acknowledged the centrality of the religious spirit in giving birth to America. As John Adams put it in 1818, "The Revolution was effected before the war commenced. [It] was in the minds and hearts of the people; a change in their religious sentiments of their duties and obligations." He saw religion, indeed, as the foundation of the American civic spirit:

> One great advantage of the Christian religion is that it brings the great principle of the law of nature and nations, love your neighbour as yourself, and do to others as you would that others do to you, to the knowledge, belief and veneration of the whole people. Children, servants, women and men are all professors in the science of public as well as private morality. .... The duties and rights of the man and the citizen are thus taught from early infancy.

The United States of America was not, therefore, a secular state; it might more accurately be described as a moral and ethical society without a state religion. Clearly, those who created it saw it as an entity, to use Lincoln's later phrase, "under God." The Declaration of Independence in its first paragraph invokes "the Laws of Nature and of Nature's God" as the entitlement of the American people to choose separation, and it insists that men have the right to "Life, Liberty and the pursuit of Happiness" because they are so "endowed by their Creator." The authors appeal, in their conclusion, to "the Supreme Judge of the world" and express their confidence in "the Protection of Divine Providence."

Equally, those who were called to govern the new state saw it as a political society within a religious framework. Washington began his first inaugural address (1789) with a prayer to "that Almighty Being, who rules over the universe, who presides in the councils of nations," asking him to bless a government consecrated "to the liberties and happiness of the people." He added that in "tendering this homage to the great Author of every public and private good" he was certain he was expressing the sentiments of Congress as well as his own, for "no people can be bound to acknowledge and adore the invisible hand which conducts the affairs of men more than the people of the United

States. Every step by which they have advanced to the character of an independent nation seems to have been distinguished by some token of providential agency." When finally relinquishing office in 1796, Washington again expressed the wish that "Heaven may continue to you the choicest tokens of its beneficence." In a memorable passage he pointed out that "religion and morality are indispensible supports" of "political prosperity" and that the "mere politician" ought to "respect and cherish them." Nor, he added, was a purely secular morality enough in itself: "Reason and experience both forbid us to expect that national morality can prevail in exclusion of religious principle." Virtue and morality were the "necessary spring of popular government" and no one who supported it could "look with indifference upon attempts to shake the foundations of the fabric." In Washington's eyes, at least, America was in no sense a secular state.

What is still more remarkable is that during the nineteenth century the cold, secularizing wind that progressively denuded government in Europe of its religious foliage left America virtually untouched. The Civil War, like the Revolution, was the political and military expression of a religious event, the product of the second Great Awakening (ca. 1795-1835), just as the Revolution was the product of the first. Lincoln, like Washington, saw the Deity as the final arbiter of public policy, but in addition he articulated what I would call the most characteristic element in American political philosophy—the belief that the providential plan and the workings of democracy are organically linked. As he made clear in his first inaugural address (1861), the dispute between North and South, and its resolution, would illustrate the way in which the democratic process was divinely inspired:

> Why should there not be a patient confidence in the ultimate justice of the people? Is there any better or equal hope in the world? . . . If the Almighty Ruler of Nations, with his eternal truth and justice, be on your side of the North, or yours of the South, that truth and that justice will surely prevail by the judgment of this great tribunal of the American people.

He added that "intelligence, patriotism, Christianity and a firm reliance on Him who has never yet forsaken this favoured land" could still solve "our present difficulty."

When Lincoln issued the Emancipation Proclamation in

1862, he appealed both to world opinion and God for approval; or, as the text has it, "I invoke the considerate judgment of mankind and the gracious favour of Almighty God." Lincoln confided to his cabinet that the timing was determined by what he considered to be divine intervention in the Battle of Antietam. The Navy Secretary Gideon Welles noted in his diary,

> He remarked that he had made a vow—a covenant—that if God gave us the victory in the approaching battle he would consider it an indication of the Divine will, and that it was his duty to move forward in the cause of the slaves. He was satisfied it was right—and confirmed and strengthened in his action by the vow and its results.

Probably no man ever reflected more deeply on the relationship between religion and politics than Lincoln, the archetypal American statesman. To clarify his own thought, he wrote on a slip of paper,

> The will of God prevails. In great contests each party claims to act in accordance with the will of God. Both may be, and one must be, wrong. God cannot be for and against the same thing at the same time. In the present Civil War it is quite possible that God's purpose is something different from the purpose of either party; and yet the human instrumentalities, working just as they do, are of the best adaptation to effect His purpose. I am almost ready to say that this is probably true; that God wills this contest and wills that it should not end yet. By his mere great power on the minds of the now contestants, he could have either saved or destroyed the Union without a human contest. Yet the contest began. And, having begun, He could give the final victory to either side any day. Yet the contest proceeds.

These reflections he recast into a famous passage in his second inaugural address (1865). It is impossible to imagine Lincoln's European contemporaries Napoleon III, Bismarck, Gambetta, Thiers, Garibaldi, Cavour, Marx, or Disraeli thinking in these terms. Gladstone, it is true, might have done so, but he would not have ventured to publicize his thinking in a critical address—or even to his Cabinet colleagues. Lincoln did so in the certainty that most of his countrymen and women could and did think along similar lines.

It is because religion was the determining factor in the two decisive events of American history, the Revolution and the Civil War, that Americans have continued to accord it a special place in their political process, both at the popular and at the highest level. At the time of the Spanish-American War and the annexation of the Philippines, President McKinley said he was "not ashamed" to admit to a gathering of his fellow Methodists that

> I went down on my knees and prayed Almighty God for light and guidance more than one night. And one night late it came to me this way. . . . There was nothing left for us to do but to take them all and to educate the Philippinos and uplift and civilize and Christianize them, and by God's grace do the very best we could by them, as our fellow men for whom Christ also died.

No European imperialist, whether a Joe Chamberlain or a Jules Ferr or a King Leopold, would have dared to justify himself in such a manner, rightly fearing accusations of humbug. But McKinley was patently sincere; no American thought otherwise. No wonder, then, that President Wilson, the first American head of state to operate on the European scene, seemed so rich and strange a figure to European politicians. Keynes, observing him at the Versailles Peace Conference, did not see him as a politician at all: "The president was like a Nonconformist minister, perhaps a Presbyterian." He "thundered commandments from the White House," and when he came to Europe "he could have preached a sermon on any of them or have addressed a stately prayer to the Almighty for their fulfillment, but he could not frame their concrete application to the actual state of Europe." I believe Keynes's reaction was typical of Europeans. Even today, if European observers were asked to single out what they believe to be the single most pervasive characteristic of American public men in this century, I think they would point to the quasi-religious character of their rhetoric, whether that of a puritan like Coolidge or a Catholic like Kennedy, men of strong faith like Hoover and Reagan or cynics like Roosevelt and Johnson.

For the truth is, the political culture of the United States is strongly religious, and the reason why it is religious, unlike Europe's, is that the political process and the religious establishment have never been perceived to be in conflict. The harmony of religion and liberty in the United States was the first thing that struck Tocqueville. "In France," he wrote in *Democracy in America* (1835), "I had almost always seen the spirit of religion and the spirit of freedom pursuing courses diametrically opposed to each other; but in America I found that they were intimately united, and that they reigned in common over the same country." He held that religion was "the foremost of the political institutions" of America, since republican democracy, with its minimal use of authority and the power of government, could not survive without religious sanctions, voluntarily accepted. The point was reiterated 120 years later by President Eisenhower, probably as typical of mid-twentieth-century American religious attitudes as Lincoln was of those prevailing in the mid-nineteenth-century. Eisenhower told *Christian Century* in 1954 that "Our government makes no sense unless it is founded on a deeply felt religious faith." He added—and this is still more characteristic—"and I don't care what it is."

Eisenhower's indifference to credal distinctions reflected faithfully the Erasmian nature of religious America. It was and is concerned with moral conduct rather than dogma; American religious groups were judged not by their theology but by the behavior of their adherents. Thus the very diversity of the sects constituted the national religious strength, since all operated within a broad common code of morals, and their competition for souls mirrored the competition of firms for business in the market economy. In both cases the role of the state was to hold the ring and make that competition fair. The First Amendment no more made America a secular state than its antitrust legislation made it a socialist state. By the twentieth century, the American republic had come to rest on a tripod of forces: religion, democracy, and capitalism. All were mutually supportive; each would fall without the others. Indeed, any two would fall without the third. When Coolidge said that "the business of America is business," he might equally well have added "and the religion of America is religion." That was exactly what Eisenhower meant.

The positive merits of American religious pluralism explain why the growth of the state education system never became, as in Europe, a source of conflict. It was nonsectarian without being nonreligious, and its moving spirit, Horace Mann, contended that religious instruction should be taken "to the extremest verge to which it can be carried without invading those rights of conscience which are established by the laws of God, and guaranteed by the constitution of the state." In the early stages, the public schools taught a kind of generalized Protestantism as a form of "character-building." Later, as the makeup of American society broadened to include millions of Catholics and Jews, the specifically religious element was further diluted until it disappeared altogether and was succeeded by what might be called the spirituality of the Republic, itself based upon the Protestant ethical and moral consensus. So the American Way of Life came to be adopted as the official philosophy of American state education.

Jews and Catholics were able to accept the public school system and the broader national ethic it reflected because the concept of libertarian plurality in religion coincided exactly with their interests. In the 1850s the Irish, nearly all of them Catholics, constituted 35.2 percent of all immigrants, and altogether over 3.5 million of them went to America to escape Protestant government and Protestant landlordism. In 1884, for the first time in history, a leading Catholic prelate was able to endorse a state that did not accord a special status to his church:"There is no conflict between the Catholic Church and America," said Archbishop John Ireland of St. Paul, ". . . and when I assert, as I now solemnly do, that the principles of the church are in thorough harmony with the interests of the republic, I know in the depths of my soul that I speak the truth."

For immigrant Jews, the motive of religious freedom was still stronger. In the years 1881 to 1914 over two million of them came to the United States, constituting ten percent of all immigrants in the early years of the twentieth century. The overwhelming majority of them came from Russia, Rumania, and Galicia, and their primary motive was to escape systematic discrimination and active persecution on religious grounds. What attracted them to America, above all, was not its secularity but its religiosity; America was not just neutral regarding religions; it was *benevolently* neutral. For Catholics and Jews alike, America had a unique appeal: their religious practices were not merely tolerated—they were respected. Had America's open door policy been maintained in the 1930s and '40s, there is little doubt that most of the victims of the Holocaust would have found refuge there, just as in the past two decades millions of persecuted Catholics from Indochina and Cuba have equated religious freedom with American citizenship. In the 1980s, as in the days of the *Mayflower,* the United States is the first and obvious choice of anyone anywhere in the world dislocated in the cause of religious freedom. Such a country cannot accurately be described as a secular state; indeed, it is America's continuing role as the primary refuge of the persecuted that underlines its religious exceptionalism.

Equally important is the way in which the religious impulse maintains its importance in the dynamics of American public life. This has its negative as well as its positive aspects, however; for if religion is a unifying force by underpinning republicanism and democracy, it can also be a divisive one. Indeed, it is often both at the same time. The first Great Awakening inspired the Revolution and so created America. But it also divided colonial society: a quarter of the nation remained neutral; a quarter was loyalist— 40,000 of them migrated to Canada. The second Great Awakening abolished slavery and launched and won the Civil War, but in the process it tested the Union almost to destruction and left wounds that did not heal for a century. The third Great Awakening (ca. 1875-1914) produced that great, unsuccessful, and tragic experiment in social engineering Prohibition, which divided the nation in half, set town against country, Catholic against Protestant, native against immigrant, and Middle America against the rest.

What we are seeing now is a fourth Great Awakening, and it too is proving divisive in some ways. In no period has American exceptionalism been more marked, have American religious patterns diverged more sharply from those of the West as a whole, than in the twentieth century. In Europe, nearly all religions were in numerical decline by 1914, a trend never since reversed. In Britain, for instance, church attendance, as a percentage of the population, peaked in the 1880s (as did institutional atheism). In the United States, church affiliation was 43 percent of the population in 1910 and in 1920; but by 1940 it was 49 percent, rising to 55 percent in 1950 and 69 percent in 1960, then falling to 62.4 percent a decade later.

The postwar afflatus, followed by a relative decline that has continued in the mainline churches, has concealed a steady and cumulatively formidable growth in religious conservatism, most marked in the Protestant churches but by no means confined to them. The fourth Great Awakening has gathered speed slowly but now appears to be maturing. Like its predecessors, it is having political consequences, the first being the phenomenon of Reaganism and the revulsion from the liberal collectivism of the 1960s and 1970s. What seems to have happened is that as the mainline churches began to decline, they sought the mutual protection of ecumenicalism through the National and World Council of Churches and the common political platform of ever more extreme forms of liberalism. This move provoked an angry conservative response from their disenfranchised rank-and-file that took the form of a new and nonelitist variety of ecumenicalism, a de facto unity that stretches across the sects and even into Catholicism. This popular ecumenicalism is based upon a common reassertion of traditional moral values and of belief in the salient articles of Christianity not as symbols but as plain historical facts. What is unusual about this fourth Awakening is that for the first time it embraces Catholics. Indeed, it appeals to many nonpracticing Christians, and even non-Christians who feel that the Judeo-Christian system of ethics and morals that underlies American republican democracy is in peril and in need of reestablishment. The phenomenon has no counterpart in Europe. It reminds us that religion and politics are organically linked in America, movements in one echoing and reinforcing movements in the other. Just as the strength of religion in America sustains and nurtures democracy, so the vigorous spirit of American democracy continually reinforces popular religion. Thus, while America remains the world's most powerful and enthusiastic champion of democracy, it is likely to preserve its exceptional role as the citadel of voluntary religion.

Secular and Religious America

Everett Carll Ladd

What do we know, comparatively, about the religious beliefs and practices of Americans? How does the American religious experience compare with that of other countries, especially other advanced industrial democracies, and how do present American religious beliefs and practices compare with those of times past? These questions are related to a persistent scholarly interest in the complex relationships among socioeconomic development, modernization and "modernity," "secularism," and religion. A quarter century ago there was something approaching consensus on the emergence of "secular America"—that is, the assumption that America had entered a period in which religion was in a permanent state of weakness or decline. Today, few scholars feel sure that this is so, and some feel quite the opposite. One reads that the United States is in the midst of a fourth "Great Awakening." This conference posits at least the vital possibility of "unsecular America."

I have been asked to review what survey research has to say on this important confluence of issues. Such a responsibility is easily discharged. Opinion research says what it can about this subject clearly and unambiguously. On the other hand, there are

---

The author wishes to express his appreciation to John Benson, Marianne Simonoff, and Lynn Zayachkiwsky for their work on this paper.

severe limits on what polls can tell us. They are blunt instruments. Sufficient to locate religious beliefs in a general comparative context, they cannot help us much with the searching, the ambiguity, the depth and subtlety that inevitably surround so basic a set of human needs and values. This should not be taken as a criticism of polling itself but simply as a caution against assuming that structured opinion research might offer a complete understanding of complex, variegated belief systems.

There is another, very different reason why we quickly exhaust what survey research has to tell us about the issue before this conference: the factors contributing to the misunderstandings that dominate the literature have little to do with the availability or the deficiencies of polling information; they are, instead, conceptual. I want to say something about my understanding of this conceptual problem, but first, I think we should briefly review the survey findings.

THE UNITED STATES COMPARED TO OTHER COUNTRIES

A great many observers have noted that, religiously, the United States does not behave as it "should," given its economic, technological, scientific, "postindustrial" development. Political scientist Walter Dean Burnham observed in 1981 that "the proposition suggests itself that the higher the level of development in a given society (the closer it is to the 'advanced industrial society' end of a developmental continuum), the smaller will be the fraction of its population for whom religious beliefs are of great importance."[1] Testing this proposition, Burnham assessed a large number of countries in terms of their degree of economic development (measured by some twenty-two "development variables") and the extent to which their citizens profess that their religious beliefs are important or unimportant in their lives. "Two things are immediately visible on inspection," Burnham notes. "First, the overall relationship is not only as posited, it is nearly linear and extremely strong"—that is, the more "developed" the country, the less important its citizens tend to consider religion. "Sec-

---

1. Burnham, "The 1980 Earthquake: Realignment, Reaction, or What?" in *The Hidden Election: Politics and Economics in the 1980 Presidential Campaign,* ed. Thomas Ferguson and Joel Rogers (New York: Pantheon Books, 1981), p. 132.

ond, the United States in particular does not fit the main sequence at all." Burnham's findings plot a very nice regression line along which most countries are clustered—and then there is the United States way off in a corner, highly developed and very religious. Burnham's statistical rendering of this ostensible conundrum is interesting, but of course the basic condition has been noted and effectively described by a number of writers. We have, in particular, S. M. Lipset's splendid summary in his book *The First New Nation*, in which he notes that foreign observers have long been struck by the strength of religious beliefs and practice in the United States. Summarizing a number of different kinds of data, Lipset concludes that "the one empirical generalization which does seem justified about American religion is that from the early nineteenth century down to the present, the United States has been among the most religious countries in the Christian world."[2]

A major survey of social values conducted in 1981 by Gallup affiliates in many countries around the world provides the most complete recent data on this question. I have brought together a large body of material from these cross-national surveys, comparing the United States to thirteen European nations (see Table 1 on pp. 115-26). Whatever the dimension examined— church membership, attendance, voluntary work for religious organizations, religious participation through prayer, the sense of drawing strength from religion, a belief in a personal God, or various other commitments—the United States appears consistently at or near the top of the field as the "most religious" nation. The Scandanavian countries and other northern European nations such as France and West Germany dominate the other end of this continuum. The results of this 1981 investigation are generally consistent with the findings of previous Gallup surveys, including those done thirteen years earlier (see Table 2 on p. 127).

By just about every measure that survey researchers have conceived and employed, the United States appears markedly more religious than its peers in the family of nations, the other industrial democracies. This relationship was established a long

---

2. Lipset, *The First New Nation: The United States in Historical and Comparative Perspective* (1963; Garden City, N.Y.: Doubleday-Anchor, 1967), pp. 170-71.

time ago. Available measures do not allow us to make the assertion confidently, but it is quite possible that the extent of the United States's religious differentiation from other industrial countries may have increased in recent years; we can say confidently that it has not decreased. Why is the United States so consistently different?

Lipset has emphasized "the effect of the separation of church and state, which resulted in American churches being voluntary organizations in which congregational self-government was the predominant form of church government."[3] Religious denominations have clearly drawn on the extraordinary power of American liberal individualism.

In *Democracy in America*, Alexis de Tocqueville remarks on the general strength of voluntary associations in the United States. Americans were a nation of joiners. He explained this propensity in terms of individualism: "The citizen of the United States is taught from infancy to rely upon his own exertions in order to resist the evils and the difficulties of life; he looks upon the social authority with an eye of mistrust and anxiety, and he claims its assistance only when he is unable to do without it." Joining together with other like-minded persons to meet common needs and attack common problems expresses a sense of individual responsibility and self-confidence.

> If a stoppage occurs in a thoroughfare and the circulation of vehicles is hindered, the neighbors immediately form themselves into a deliberative body; and this extemporaneous assembly gives rise to an executive power which remedies the inconvenience before anybody has thought of recurring to a pre-existing authority superior to that of the persons immediately concerned. ... In the United States associations are established to promote the public safety, commerce, industry, morality, and religion. There is no end which the human will despairs of attaining through the combined power of individuals united into a society.[4]

---

3. Lipset, *The First New Nation*, pp. 180-81.
4. Tocqueville, *Democracy in America* (1835; New York: Vintage Books, 1954), 1: 198.

A variant of this explanation notes the importance of competition and "free markets." With the establishment of a state church proscribed by the First Amendment, and government for the most part eschewing special assistance to any one of the many competing denominations, a religious equivalent of an economic free market resulted—only more so, because the marketplace in religion has been subject to much less regulatory control and assistance than the economic marketplace. The results have followed the lines of market competition generally, the growth in this case being a more dynamic, participating denominational life. When older, established churches have lost touch with important segments of their "markets," new "firms" have been more than ready to fill the void. We have seen this worked out in the Protestant denominational experience of the past quarter century as conservative and fundamentalist churches have grown, in some cases dramatically, and the mainline churches have declined.

Outside the United States, the historic association of churches with nondemocratic forces, especially the aristocracy, meant that proponents of a newer, freer, more egalitarian and democratic order often had good reason to hold that religious institutions—and by an understandable if ultimately invalid extrapolation, religious belief—were their enemies. In contrast, the United States has historically understood that religious experience contributes to the strength and vitality of democracy.

Tocqueville's insights on one key aspect of this important story are worth reciting again. He argues that the religious beliefs and institutions the Pilgrims brought with them to New England contributed much to the vigorous democratic practice that took root long before independence was achieved from Britain. The Pilgrims thought that every individual should have a knowledge of Scripture, which meant that everyone should be able to read, and so they pioneered in establishing a compulsory system of public education. This helped make citizens more aware and better able to involve themselves in community life. Believing that every individual was equal in the eyes of God, the Pilgrims made rules, compacts, and institutions that gave each person a voice in social affairs, including government. Such beliefs were "not merely a religious doctrine, but corresponded in many points with the most absolute democratic and republican theories," says Tocqueville. In New England "a democracy, more perfect than antiquity had dared to dream of, started in full size and panoply from the midst of an ancient feudal society."[5] It is sadly the case that contemporary social science has chosen not to build upon, or even concur with the stark brilliance of Tocqueville's insight into the relationship of religion and "modernity" in colonial New England. He saw that "the Americans have succeeded in incorporating to some extent one with the other and combining admirably" two distinct elements—"the *spirit of religion* and the *spirit of liberty.* The settlers of New England were at the same time ardent sectarians and daring innovators."

Religious belief has both contributed to and accommodated the dominant American ideology. Since the ratification of the Constitution two centuries ago, a great orienting ideology has dominated American thought. It is rooted in classical liberalism, but since it has never received a statement in classical liberal thought outside the United States comparable to what it has received here, we are justified in calling it simply "the American ideology." This philosophy's intellectual ascendancy and the extent to which its vision has crowded out every alternative have been nicely described by many scholars.[6] Observers of American politics have often commented on the ideology's striking persistence during two centuries in which so much else has changed. A socially dynamic America has in this sense been a conservative nation, seeking throughout its history to maintain and extend established values rather than pursue new ones. And observers have noted a similar phenomenon in the persistent vitality of religion here even in the face of developments that elsewhere have disrupted religious belief.

The source of the continuity is much the same in both cases. A set of values present in the colonial experience led to the establishment of a consistent set of social and political institutions. Inextricably linked, these institutions and values have been endorsed by every subsequent generation of Americans—although obviously not by every group equally. Thus reinforced, they have persisted. "America is the only nation in the world that

---

5. Tocqueville, *Democracy in America,* 1: 32-47, *passim.*
6. See in particular Louis Hartz, *The Liberal Tradition in America* (Boston: Houghton-Mifflin, 1955).

is founded on a Creed," G. K. Chesterton observed.[7] Religious
beliefs are interwoven in that creed and reflect its central values,
including commitments to individualism, equality, and freedom.
The pronounced religiousness of Americans compared to citizens of other industrial democracies is to some degree part and
parcel of the unique commitment Americans have made over
two change-filled centuries to a defining, domineering ideology.

The persistence of religious belief in the United States
makes an important point—namely, that the common assumption that industrial and postindustrial development are inherently
disruptive of religion is simply wrong. Aspects of the social and
political experience obviously led to a decline of religious belief
and practice in a number of industrial countries, but it was not
the processes of development per se that brought about this
decline. The United States has not repealed or confounded the
laws of history; it has simply arrived at modernity through a route
different from that followed by most other countries. This has
had important consequences for a lot of America's institutions,
including its Madisonian polity, its private-property-based economy, and its dynamic, competitive, democratic, individualistic
religious institutions.

HISTORICAL CONTINUITY

Lipset argued in 1963 against any interpretation of American
religious experience that posits a simple straight-line progression
toward becoming either more or less religious over time. "Although there have been ebbs and flows in enthusiasm," he says,
"basic long-term changes in formal religious affiliation and practice have not occurred."[8] Survey data collected during the past
twenty years add further support to this conclusion. Although
ebbs and flows can be seen, the underlying continuity is most
impressive. Tables 3-7 on pages 128-31 show stability in rates of
church attendance, in public confidence in religious institutions,
and in the sense of religion's importance. Table 8 (p. 131) does
suggest that since the early 1960s, large numbers of Americans
have felt that religion is losing influence in national life, but this

---

7. Chesterton, *What I Saw in America* (New York: Dodd, Mead,
1922), pp. 7-8.
8. Lipset, *The First New Nation,* p. 170.

probably reflects that the anxiety people typically feel about the status of a valued institution or belief, rather than objective evidence of religion's decline. Looking at attitudes toward work, for instance, one sees all kinds of indications that the work ethic is alive and well despite the fact that large numbers of people worry that their fellow citizens don't have the same commitment they had in the past.

The fact is that as Tables 9-15 show (see pp. 132-37), Americans continue to profess a strikingly high commitment to religion. Over seventy percent of a national sample interviewed by Yankelovich, Skelly, and White in September 1983 went so far as to state that they would not vote for a presidential candidate who did not believe in God, "even if [they] really liked him and . . . shared his political views" (see Table 10, p. 132). Of those interviewed by the National Opinion Research Center in 1983 and 1984 as part of the General Social Surveys, about fifty-five percent said that they typically pray at least once a day. The 1984 NORC survey found huge majorities professing traditional views of God and the Bible—for example, the view that the Bible is either the literal or the inspired word of God, not an "ancient book of fables, legends, history, and moral precepts recorded by men" (see Table 12, p. 134).

Having cited all the results of these polls, I think it is important to repeat the caution that polls are blunt instruments. The data I have presented are about as good as survey research is likely to yield on the topic before us. But obviously polls cannot look into people's hearts, learn everything about what they really think, or measure the true depth and conviction of their religious experience. And, indeed, there are those who claim that religious beliefs were actually more vital in the past than they are now, despite what the crude "objective" data available to us indicate. But I think they are wrong. Polling data may not plumb the spiritual depths of those questions, but I am convinced that they map the contours of the nation's attitudes with some accuracy.

I suspect that religious belief and practice have always left a good bit to be desired so far as depth and sincerity are concerned. Nevertheless, by all conventional measures, Americans are a fairly religious people compared to their counterparts in other industrial countries, and they have been a religious people throughout their history. Of course one can always lament the incompleteness or insincerity of this religion, and it is true that for those who are directly involved, the ebbs and flows in American religious belief and practice may well be enormously important. But the essential findings of the social scientist are not challenged by minor short-term changes any more than they're challenged by groundless anxieties about the decline of religion or nostalgic recollections of good old days of fervent belief that in fact never existed. The findings indicate a continuity of strong religious commitment in America relative to other industrial nations.

GROUP DIFFERENCES IN RELIGIOUS PRACTICE AND BELIEF

Some analysts concur with the general conclusions we have reached thus far but then insist that the generalization obscures a crucial underlying diversity. As a whole the American people are religious, they concede, but this whole is made up of some groups who are extremely religious in traditional American and even "premodern" terms, and other groups that have pretty much given up on religion. Averaging it all out, one gets a fairly religious whole, but according to the critics such averaging is a specious exercise.

This argument has appeared in a number of different forms. Some contend that religious commitment has changed with the generations, that young people have a strikingly different worldview than their elders. Another interpretation emphasizes the importance of education as a dividing line, arguing that college-trained individuals, and especially the younger people in this group, tend to be vastly more "secular" than the older people who have received only grade school and high school educations. Yet a third group has argued that religious people are disproportionately "underclass," ethnic, and marginal, and that cosmopolitan America is on the whole a good deal more secular.

But the data refute these arguments. Tables 16-25 (on pp. 138-48) show the professed religious practices and values of various subgroups making up the American population. I spend a lot of time comparing groups in their social and political commitments, and I am struck by how modest the group differences often are in the "core" area of religion. Of course styles change and some (especially the young and the college-trained) are more likely to pick up on the new styles than others (especially the old and those less exposed to "cosmopolitan" influences). But to the extent that Tables 16-25 capture underlying dimensions of religious practice and values—and I think they do this fairly well—they show that American religiousness cuts strikingly across group lines. Many people would probably be surprised by how little difference there is on many fundamental religious matters from one social group to another—because in the area of social values generally these groups are much more significantly opposed one to another. I will return to this point shortly, but first I want to relate another part of the story.

A RELIGIOUS AND SECULAR PEOPLE

My argument is that America is today what it has always been: a highly religious, intensely secular society. Nothing much seems to be happening on either of these fronts—the latter because we have gone about as far as we can go; the former because we see no reason to back away from the point we long ago arrived at. Martin Marty has suggested (correctly, I believe) that the kaleidoscopic shifts in religious belief and institutional experience in the United States during the past several decades have occurred "within the borders of an 'all-pervasive religiousness' and a concurrent and 'persistent secularity.' "[9] He refers to the "religio-secular" character of America's most fundamental commitments. "The double paradigm will no doubt diminish the audaciousness of certain prophecies and projections: bold predictions of the purely secular city or a thoroughly sacral culture are obviously highly dramatic."[10] I would put the matter a little differently. Our dual status—as both religious and secular—is sometimes described as confusing and contradictory. In fact, it isn't contradictory, and it shouldn't confuse us.

My dictionary's first definition of secularism is "a system of political or social philosophy that rejects all forms of religious faith." According to this definition, the United States obviously cannot be at once both highly religious and highly secular. But the definition is a bad one—bad in the sense that it ignores an

9. Marty, "Religion in America since Mid-Century," Daedalus, Winter 1982, p. 151.
10. Marty, "Religion in America since Mid-Century," p. 157.

important historical progression that is appropriately understood as "secularization."[11] This confusion over the meaning of a key term has contributed much to confusion over the key issue of what the necessary effects of modernity on religion actually are. To understand secularization we have to take into account a considerable number of developments stretching from the fifteenth through the eighteenth centuries. Of prime importance are three great interrelated sets of revolutionary changes: (1) the commercial, and later the industrial revolution, which dramatically expanded the wealth of nations; (2) the Enlightenment and subsequently the scientific revolution, which greatly altered our perceptions of ourselves and the universe; and (3) the egalitarian revolution that brought down ascriptive class societies and established more open, participatory, and sometimes even democratic systems in their stead. It was this whole complex process that led to the formulation of the fundamental meaning of secularization.

The transition from agricultural to industrial societies in the West brought about a major expansion in resources. This upset the conditions under which millions had been willing to acquiesce to extensive privileges for a few from which they and their children were formally and permanently excluded. Only when there is in fact no possibility of most people living beyond bare subsistence will the majority patiently consent to the existence of an arbitrarily selected privileged elite. The rule of an aristocracy is tenable only in scarcity-bound societies. Let the pie dramatically expand—which is what economic-technological developments caused to happen in the seventeenth and eighteenth centuries—and groups of people outside the hereditary privileged class will step forward to claim their share, will come to feel that life owes them something other than perpetual wretchedness. With the prospect of continuing growth in economic output, it became more realistic to suggest, as Jefferson did in the American Declaration of Independence, that all people have a birthright to the vigorous pursuit of earthly happiness.

The idea that people, even regular people, have a right to

---

11. I understand that a great many angels have danced on the head of this pin. For some of the different usages of the terms *secular* and *secularization,* see Larry Shiner, "The Meanings of Secularization," in *Secularization and the Protestant Prospect,* ed. James F. Childress and David B. Harned (Philadelphia: Westminster, 1970), pp. 30-42.

expect happiness *in this world* is a key part of the concept of secularization. It became possible to view people in a wholly new light, as sovereign beings with rights as well as duties. "Individualism," says Tocqueville, "is a novel expression, to which a novel idea has given birth." Individualism is a luxury of societies that find it possible to escape the absolute domination of scarcity.

There was a continuing interaction between physical and psychological processes, between events and ideas. The economic stirrings of industrialization created new expectations. Masses of people came to believe that they could change the way they lived, and the idea of progress as we know it now took form. Society became more and more secularized, more and more oriented to this world, as energies were channeled into altering the here and now.

The new ways of viewing man's psychological apparatus that were formulated in the West during the seventeenth and eighteenth centuries, provided the intellectual underpinnings of individualism. The best scientific thought pictured the brain as a simple Newtonian machine. Ideas were assumed to come from the senses, and it was held that the job of the brain is to organize the sensations brought to it. The implication of this was that if the input (the sensations drawn from the individual's environment) could be controlled, then the output (the way people think and perceive, and indeed the type of people they are) could be determined. If this brain, this simple machine, is approximately the same for all people, then output is different (i.e., people are different) only because the input varies. The brain, Locke wrote, is at birth an "empty cabinet," a *tabula rasa* "void of all characters, without any ideas," and what we become depends on what our environment writes on the empty slate. This was an extraordinarily secularizing idea. The sensationalist epistemology of Locke and his contemporaries was earthshaking in its time. The suggestion that people are approximately equal in natural capabilities, that they differ only because the environments of some are better than those of others, undercut any rationale for the permanent privilege of the aristocracy. Aristocrats were simply people blessed with better environments. In sum, just as the economic expansion of the industrial revolution created the material basis for the assumption that life had something beyond gross deprivation for the average person, the intellectual basis for a thoroughly secular individualism was developed from a view of human psychology that attributed performance to environment.

As the scientific revolution advanced, naturalistic explanations of the way the world works were gradually extended, finding acceptance in the general public. For example, it was determined that people get sick because nasty little microbes afflict their bodies, not because of mysterious and fundamentally unknowable forces. In its extreme form, philosophic naturalism holds that *all* objects and events can be accounted for by scientific explanation, that there are no nonnatural objects, processes, or causes. But of course, only a few scientistic ideologues have ever believed this. For most people, the extension of naturalistic reasoning simply meant that a lot of objects and events could be accounted for by scientific explanation, often to substantial human benefit.

The United States was born at the juncture of these many revolutionary changes, and American values and outlook have from the outset been dominated by them. The United States has never been divided between "secularized" and "premodern" segments. Virtually everyone has been comfortable with naturalistic explanations of a lot of daily life, committed to the idea of progress, insistent on a right to earthly happiness. For a variety of reasons, scattered individuals and groups have rejected this basic secularism—but not many. At times, social strata in decline have mounted what Nathan Glazer calls "defensive offensives" against ascendent strata, and these reactions have been construed as resistence to secularism.[12] The flap over Darwinism, extending through the sensationalized 1925 "monkey trial" in Dayton, Tennessee, is a

----

12. Glazer makes his observations about a "defensive offensive" in a narrower context than that in which I am using the term here. He argues that the response over the last fifteen years or so of conservative Christians on such issues as abortion, school prayer, and pornography are not an aggressive attempt to impose their ethical judgments on the country so much as an expression of a limited resistence to the bold, largely successful assault by opposing interests in the 1960s and 1970s on the principle of "local option" in these areas of value choice. The principle of local option had been used to keep the peace in a pluralistic society, he argues. The striking down of a great number of divergent state laws and practices regarding school prayer, abortion, and the regulation of pornography, with the federal courts as the central instrumentality, broke this peace and prompted the losing side to go on a "defensive offensive" (see Glazer, "Toward a New Concordat?" *This World,* Summer 1982, pp. 109-18).

case in point. But in the United States there simply has never been any coherent, whole-hearted assault on the essential naturalism that underlies modern science. Most Americans have remained comfortable with a secular view of the world: we can understand a lot of it; we can, and should, seek to change it; we can expect happiness from it. If naturalism could explain everything, if science and technology could control everything, if the capacities of an industrial economy could solve all problems, then there would, arguably, be no place for religion, for belief in God, for what are sometimes referred to as the sacred and the transcendent. But the natural world offers no such panaceas. This conclusion derives not from the musings of frustrated religionists but from the cold, clearheaded reasoning of science. And this is why the most secular of societies can easily be at the same time among the most religious. William Jennings Bryan remarked that "it is better to trust in the Rock of Ages than to know the age of rock; it is better for one to know that he is close to the Heavenly Father than to know how far the stars in the heavens are apart." Well, you can't blame a fellow for letting go with a little rhetoric, but of course the whole idea is silly. Very few Americans now, fifty years ago, a hundred years ago, or two hundred years ago really believed there was any need to choose between trusting God and studying a little geology.

Religious commitments and scientific, naturalistic, secular views of the world exist side by side with little strain in most people in the United States—because they understand the inescapable limits of the latter. This doesn't stop some from taking enormous leaps, of course, and suggesting that scientific reasoning has brought them close to understanding all of the fundamental developments of the universe—all the way back to the "big bang." But these individuals remain on the fringe. Very few Americans resent carrying naturalistic reasoning as far as it can go and then granting that they are left with a large portion of life, including many of its most important dimensions, to deal with.

CONFLICTS OVER VALUES

Underlying America's "religio-secular paradigm" is a striking national consensus. As a country that has rested comfortably for two centuries with the secularism that defines modernity, the

United States is free from the profound cultural discontinuities that afflict countries whose populations are spread across different rungs of a "developmental ladder." Most groups in our population have long since reconciled, with reasonable ease, secular perspectives and religious impulses—although the ways in which these reconciliations are expressed vary enormously, and at times they may lead us to believe—incorrectly—that the variations have real substance.

All this explains why religious issues move and divide the contemporary American public as little as they do, despite intermittent efforts by some among the elite to give religion a divisive property. All the central elements for an essential harmony are in place. "Modernity" has long since gone as far as it can go. The separation of church and state, despite some rhetoric to the contrary, is universally accepted in essentially the same terms. Conflict occurs only on the margin of this broad policy area. Most Americans submit to the idea of a personal God, whom they perceive in quite traditional terms. (Of course, the usual class-related differences as to the proper manner of addressing the Deity continue to abound.) The propriety of and need for prayer, including school prayer, is widely recognized, and a very large proportion of the public favors a modest rollback of court rulings (e.g., in *Engel v. Vitale* [1962] and related cases) to provide a greater measure of local option with safeguards for minority sensibilities (see Table 26, pp. 149-51).

One expression of this larger religious consensus is the diminution of political divisions among religious groups—again, despite some efforts by segments of the elite to widen these divisions. For all of the talk about church and state in the 1984 campaign, most Americans were little exercised. When asked, less than ten percent of the voters reported that their clergymen had offered any encouragement to vote for either Reagan or Mondale, and such partisan urgings as were made from the pulpit were evenly divided between the two principal candidates (see Table 27, p. 152). And, of course, almost no one paid much attention to such efforts when they were made. America has a history of religious groups voting in sharp opposition one to another, reflecting important social tensions organized around religious group lines. But in 1984 the differences among religious groups in presidential preference were modest indeed, probably the least substantial in American history (see Table 28, p. 153).

Of course the American public remains divided, sometimes sharply so, over a number of political issues that involve contrasting social values and perspectives. Abortion is a good example. After a decade in which the statutes of fifty states were stricken by a Supreme Court decision (*Roe v. Wade,* 1973), and perhaps fifteen million abortions have been performed nationally, it is hardly surprising that passions are aroused. Both sides to the conflict see morality on their side. Both express their moral convictions in terms of fundamental individual rights—although here as in other instances the antagonists are separated by a wide gulf on the question of *which* individuals and which rights need greater recognition. As Table 29 shows (see p. 154), group differences on this issue are large and easily located. Various teachings, including those derived from churches and colleges, along with class-related differences in expectations account for the contrasting perspectives on what reverence for the individual requires.

A very large segment of the general public finds itself cross-pressured and torn by the issue of abortion. When the issue is framed in terms of the individual woman being given a choice— "Do you agree or disagree [that] . . . the decision to have an abortion should be left to the woman and her physician"—the overwhelming majority comes down on the "pro-choice" side. But only a fifth or so of the public believes that abortion should be legal under all circumstances, and three-fifths want greater restrictions than presently apply (see Table 30, pp. 155-58). Abortion is a major political issue involving important ethical concerns on which different groups in the population can "quote scripture" from America's individualistic ideology.

But, as important as abortion and similar issues are, they have little to do with the status of religion in the society or with "secularization." Strong "secular" cases are made both for and against abortion. And even avowedly religious people disagree on what policy should be. Many religious leaders have strong opinions, as they should, but the way America resolves this issue is at heart a matter of how it will resolve the powerful ethical ambiguities that continually arise from its two-centuries-old commitment to a liberating yet befuddling individualism.

Peter Berger, who seems at times to use the term *secularization* to mean antagonism "to the dimension of transcendence in the human condition," wonders "whether modernization *without* secularization is possible in different cultural contexts."[13] But of course we know the answer. The cultural context—resulting from contrasting historical experiences—is very different in Sweden than in the United States. And these two very modern countries differ enormously in the strength of their religious institutions and beliefs. "Modernity" does not inevitably establish some inescapable progression of religious decline. The experience of the United States makes that clear.

---

13. Berger, *Facing Up To Modernity: Excursions in Society, Politics, and Religion* (New York: Basic Books, 1977), p. 78.

Are Secularists the Threat?
Is Religion the Solution?

George M. Marsden

I have been asked to write this paper on "the resistance to 'the religious factor' " among some of the culturally elite, and especially their "attachment to the notion of America's being a secular or secularizing society." This assignment is based, I take it, on the observation that secularization advances not only as an impersonal sociological process but also as a cause that some people promote. Furthermore, the assumption of the assignment is that the true reasons for the championing of secularism are sufficiently hidden from view as to call for explanation.

It is not clear to me that the motives of secularists are all that obscure, so I suspect that my examination of them may be more obvious than we all would like. Nonetheless, this subject is of interest to me as a student of American evangelicalism and fundamentalism, since a less sophisticated version of the same question—the "secular humanism" conspiracy thesis—has become popular in those circles during the past decade. As a more-or-less traditionalist evangelical Christian myself, I want to ask how we should understand the viewpoint and goals of those who are promoting secularism. Are they a threat to the republic? Are they a threat to traditional Christianity? Should we simply oppose such secularists, or is there room for cooperation on public issues? Should we respond to those who promote a more secular society by promoting more religion in public life? All these, I think, are interesting questions that grow out of an initial consideration of what promoters of secularism are up to.

* * *

The proponents of a secular culture constitute a large and diverse category, and I am not sure that we can generalize about them adequately. Nevertheless, we have to try to make sense of even complex reality, so I will try to analyze secularists in terms of an ideal type. We immediately run into a major ambiguity here, however. If we mean by *secularization* simply the removal of a theistic religious reference from some aspect of human activity and by *secularists* those who champion the advance of secularization, then it should be clear that such individuals need not be anti-religious; they need only think that the society will be healthier if religion is more privatized. So, for instance, Isaac Backus, a Baptist leader at the time of the American Revolution, was a secularist in that he championed the disestablishment of state churches. As an evangelist, however, he worked against the secularization of some other aspects of society. Similarly, an evangelical Christian in early Utah might have favored most forms of secularization in that state. For similar reasons, practicing Jews might promote many forms of secularization in strongly Christian parts of the nation.

For the moment, however, let us simply grant that the advocates of a secular or secularizing society are a diverse group including lots of religious people and then proceed to focus our discussion on those who do not affirm or practice a traditional religion. This still leaves a large and diverse group of secularists, but it establishes parameters in which we can reasonably narrow the focus yet further to an ideal type that is something like the "secular humanists" of whom fundamentalists talk. We can look for something like the prevailing opinions among those influential groups in America who are not traditionally religious. Once we have assessed secularism in this purest form, we will be in a better position to say something about its theistic forms as well.

On the face of it, nontheistic secularists appear to have enormous influence in American society. Their philosophy seems to control a number of crucial opinion-forming centers. In the universities, nontheistic secularism is unquestionably the overwhelmingly dominant opinion. So also in the media. Many government agencies operate on the basis of these secularist assumptions. So does most of American business, based as it is almost solely on pragmatic principles of maximizing profits, subject to only minimal moral or religious review. American public education also reflects many of the secularist principles. The principles of nontheistic secularism, in fact, seem to be far more dominant in American society than we might expect in light of the relatively small number of people who explicitly articulate those principles. This immediately brings us to an interesting question: If Americans are such a professedly religious people, why is it that the centers of American culture are dominated by secularist principles? Fundamentalists have suggested that this is evidence of a secular humanist conspiracy. Tim LaHaye, for instance, maintains that 275,000 secular humanists control the American media, government, unions, and universities.[1]

It may indeed be true that nontheistic secularists have disproportionate influence in American life, but if they do it is not because of any well-organized conspiracy. Although nontheistic secularists do sometimes organize and have some influence, the illusion of a much wider impact is created because they speak explicitly and forcefully for an ideal that is typically held by a large number of religious people as well—namely, that public business is best conducted according to objective scientific principles (to use the term *scientific* broadly) without any reference to religious or spiritual considerations—what Jacques Ellul describes as the "technological principle." The overwhelming and all-pervasive force in modern society, says Ellul, is the principle of finding the most rational and efficient technique to get the job done. Everything falls to the onslaught of this principle.[2] Ellul may overstate his case, but even with qualifications it is a strong case. Nowhere is it better illustrated than in the American business community. With very few exceptions, professedly religious people do not manage their businesses any differently than antireligious secularists manage theirs. In each case the bottom line is finding the most efficient technique to maximize profits. Moral considerations are far down the list in determining policy.

---

1. La Haye, *The Battle for the Mind* (Old Tappan, N.J.: Revell, 1980), p. 141.
2. See Ellul, *The Technological Society* (1954; New York: Vintage Books, 1964), p. xxv.

Similar principles determine most of the conduct of government. In foreign policy, for instance, we only have to substitute "national interest" for "profits" to find the bottom line. In domestic affairs, where the views of various interest groups must be considered, ethical considerations are more often expressed, though it would be naive to suppose that they often play a primary role in policy-making.

The case of the media is well known. The market determines the content. Whatever the professed religiosity of the American people, their behavior indicates satisfaction with entertainments that are thoroughly secular and often subversive of traditional Judeo-Christian morality. Here the extent of the influence of an elite becomes more apparent. Occasionally individuals with an interest in reforming ethical standards (e.g., Norman Lear) successfully use the media to propagandize for their views.[3] Such opinions find strong support in the industry from those whose personal lifestyle inclines them to attack traditional religion and morality as a means of promoting permissiveness, especially sexual permissiveness. Such preaching is limited by what the public will stand for. But even though there is less of this sort of explicit propagandizing in the 1980s than in the 1970s, it is clear that the public will still stand for a lot. I overheard a game show the other day on which the host asked a contestant, "Of one-hundred strippers surveyed, how many will say that they can twirl their tassels?" It is not simply a sinister plot of secular humanists against the public that has produced programming of this sort. The fact is that sex sells. Millions of people watch these shows. Who is it that fills the demand? A combination of the business-oriented elite who control the industry (which includes many of the sorts of people who created Las Vegas); some artists, writers, and directors who may be anti-religious and pro-permissive; and, not incidentally, the rules of the market, which are determined by the scientific principles of what will sell.

---

3. That the problem is not a lack of concern about questions of morality is indicated by a recent study indicating that two out of three TV executives think that TV should be used to promote social reform. One person's social-moral reform may be another person's secularism, of course. See George Barna and William Paul McKay, *Vital Signs: Emerging Social Trends and the Future of American Christianity* (Westchester, Ill.: Crossway, 1984), p. 57.

In academia, another cultural domain where nontheistic secularism reigns, we find a somewhat different combination of forces. Here the market is a factor, but more a factor toward forcing the curricula in increasingly practical-technological directions. This is a secularizing factor, but not the major one. Rather, in academia we find that an anti-theistic ideal has become an article of faith and shaped the structures of institutions and of the academic disciplines themselves. I will refer to this ideal as *positivism*, using the term in a broad sense to refer to the belief that the scientific method of examining purely natural causes is the best route to knowledge, providing the best principles for the conduct of all but a few human cultural activities. Positivism in this sense has determined the very shape of the academic disciplines. As is often lamented, but seldom corrected, even the potentially humane disciplines are organized in imitation of the natural sciences. As it stands, most of the energies of people in academia are directed toward resolving technical questions of direct interest to only a small group of experts in the subdiscipline of their field.[4] The social sciences are in even more lamentable condition, combining such specialized isolation with an arcane "scientific" language, and often laboring under the assumption that they must adopt empirical approaches in direct imitation of natural sciences.[5]

Behind such arrangements is a worldview that has grown out of the observation that in the natural sciences and in related technical applications, the most productive approach to knowledge has involved isolating oneself from religious and moral commitments. This isolation, I should hasten to add and to emphasize, can be purely methodological. When scientists enter the laboratory, they can leave their religious commitments outside solely for the purpose of isolating the technical problem at hand, much as they might hang up, but not abandon, their hats and coats. As

---

4. Jacques Barzun recently expressed this view in his essay "Scholarship versus Culture," *Atlantic Monthly*, November 1984, pp. 93-104.

5. Mary Stewart Van Leeuwen notes how psychology has been placed in bondage to this standard; see *The Sorceror's Apprentice: A Christian Looks at the Changing Face of Psychology* (Downers Grove, Ill.: InterVarsity, 1982).

a methodology for dealing with certain technical questions, this seems a commendable approach. We might hope that auto mechanics would not seriously consider spiritual forces as possibly decisive in their diagnoses of what is wrong with the cars they work on. In the late nineteenth century this compelling scientific-technological methodology came widely to be regarded as the proper basis for all worldviews. The revolution is most apparent in American academia, which within a generation around the turn of the century entirely banished the religious reference that had previously set much of its basic academic agenda.

This revolution was not simply a matter of a secularized intellectual elite adopting an ideal that separated them from an essentially traditionalist culture, however. The situation was more complex. Academics were able to transform the positivist methodology into a positivist worldview so easily only because what they were doing paralleled so much else that was occurring in the culture. During the decades following 1860, in which American scientists were eagerly embracing Darwinism as a means of freeing the study of nature from reference to questions about God's design, industrialists such as Andrew Carnegie were revolutionizing industry by systemizing it according to the scientific principles of efficiency. The completion of the secularization of science, which now purported to be able to explain the development of mind and apparent design in the universe, was symbolically an important step in a process that was already well advanced. Positivism, which already dominated many of the practical affairs of the civilization, could now be advanced more plausibly as a worldview. Many scientists retained traditional religious beliefs, although for a time in the early twentieth century many did not.[6] Probably more of the leaders of business and industry remained religious (John D. Rockefeller, Sr., might serve as a type in this regard). But the point is that if there was such wide agreement that the positivist or technological methodologies (which are

---

6. James H. Leuba documents the erosion of faith among college students and especially among biologists in *The Belief in God and Immortality: A Psychological, Anthropological and Statistical Study* (Chicago: Open Court, 1921). James Turner presents a good overview of the complexity of factors in the late nineteenth-century crisis of faith in *Without God, without Creed: The Origins of Unbelief in America* (Baltimore: The Johns Hopkins University Press, 1985).

equivalent in effect) should be applied to one's professionalized field, those who wanted to transform the methodology into a worldview already had much of the way cleared for them.

The rise of the positivist-technological worldview brought with it its opposite, which could also be characterized as a version of secularism. As many people have observed, modern ideologies tend to oscillate between two poles—in this case, naturalistic determinism on the one hand and radical assertions of human freedom and autonomy on the other. The seeds of these two tendencies were present already in the Enlightenment and in the rise of romanticism in the eighteenth century. They could have grown into either theistic or nontheistic forms. Probably the combination of positivist and technological methodologies was the most significant of the forces that cleared theism from the picture by the late nineteenth century; but the nontheistic secularism of the twentieth century has been expressed in positivist and radical freedom/individualist forms, and even more often in a combination of the two forms.

In addition to these ideological factors, there were of course many social factors connected with modernization that contributed to secularization. For our purposes, one of the most important of these developments was the pluralization of American society. In the same era when positivism and the technological principle were extending their domains, traditionally dominant evangelical Christianity had to retreat from its cultural hegemony in the face of the legitimate public interests of other religious groups. This forced retreat was consistent with the principles of the anti-establishment strand in American constitutional principles, and so it did not require as wrenching an adjustment as it might have for an official religious establishment. But it is also true that the decline of evangelical Protestantism as a major culture-shaping voice was a revolutionary development that evangelicals themselves did not always accept with equanimity, as the history of fundamentalism continues to illustrate.

We can consider the outlook and motives of twentieth-century secularists, then, in the context of these broad developments (which, of course, do not exhaust the factors involved). Characteristically, nontheistic secularists hold the view that theistic beliefs reflect retarded social or personal development and that they ought to be replaced with positivist views, countervailing assertions of human freedom, or some combination of these.

Probably John Dewey can be taken as the archtypical and the most influential of such nontheistic secularists in twentieth-century America. As Henry Steele Commager, who could remember the era, said, "he became the guide, the mentor, and the conscience of the American people: it is scarcely an exaggeration to say that for a generation no major issue was clarified until Dewey had spoken.[7]

Dewey held an essentially Comtean view of the progress of human thought and civilizations from lower theological and metaphysical stages to a higher scientific stage. Just as natural science progressed when it was "no longer the slave of metaphysical and theological purpose,"[8] so philosophy and social thought should take similar steps. Humanity, Dewey recognized, was innately religious. But traditional religions, which posited scientifically dubious assertions about deities, were not the healthiest expressions of the human religious character. He urged humanity, and specifically Americans, to adopt "a common faith," a public philosophy based on a morality that valued human growth in learning, knowledge, the arts, conscience, character, and the furtherance of mutual aid and affection.[9] This moral philosophy was, of course, what Dewey hoped would be taught in the public schools, which (as is often observed) served in effect as the established church of his religion. Indeed, Dewey was more frank than most secularists in admitting the religious nature of his secular scheme. He correctly saw that secularization involved the replacement of one religion with another.

Dewey lived in the era of secularist triumphalism. His own outlook is clarified if we realize that he was a Calvinist at heart. As Bruce Kuklick has been pointing out lately, the continuities of American thought become much clearer if we realize that Dewey was reared and educated in nineteenth-century Vermont,

---

7. Commager, *The American Mind* (New Haven: Yale University Press, 1950), p. 100.
8. John Dewey, "Science in the Reconstruction of Philosophy" (1920), in *Sources of the American Mind II,* ed. Loren Baritz (New York: Joseph Wiley, 1966), p. 19. Cf. *A Common Faith* (New Haven: Yale University Press, 1934), pp. 72-73.
9. Dewey, *A Common Faith,* p. 56.

still a heartland of the New Divinity, the last flowering of Puritan theology, the most formidable tradition in American thought.[10] Until he was in his early thirties, Dewey was writing for evangelical and New Divinity journals. As the mentor of intellectual and secular Americans of the twentieth century, he shared with his audience the common experience of having been brought up in an evangelical ethos and having rejected it. This was a powerful factor in the anti-theism of a whole generation trying to free itself from a stifling evangelical conscience. But Dewey represented many of the positive aspirations of that generation as well. He still retained the Puritan ideal that there ought to be a standing religious order that provided a common moral base for the social order.

Anti-theistic secularism in this triumphalist mode does appear to be an organized effort to bring forth the cultural dominance of its secularist ideology at the expense of traditional religions. Particularly useful for interpreting this movement have been the *Humanist Manifesto* I (1933) and II (1973), those favorites so often quoted in fundamentalist attacks on "secular humanism." They are so seldom cited in any other context that one wonders if they are not like Ethan Allen's anti-Christian tracts that were hardly noticed until Timothy Dwight's polemics made them famous. Nonetheless, the manifestos do illustrate that a number of influential American thinkers have held the view that (as the 1933 document puts it) "the universe depicted by modern science makes unacceptable any supernatural or cosmic guarantees of human values," and that (as the more chastened 1973 version puts it) "reason and intelligence are the most effective instrument that humankind possesses." So "the controlled use of scientific methods . . . must be extended further in the solution of human problems."[11] Particularly in the 1933 document, where John Dewey's hand is evident, the goal is religious (their outlook

---

10. See Kuklick, "Is American Philosophy Based on a Mistake?" (Paper presented at conference on Jonathan Edwards held by the Institute for the Study of Evangelicalism in Wheaton, Illinois, October 1984) and *Churchmen and Philosophers from Jonathan Edwards to John Dewey* (New Haven: Yale University Press, 1985).

11. *Humanist Manifestos I and II* (Buffalo, N.Y.: Prometheus Books, 1973), pp. 8, 17.

is repeatedly called "religious humanism") and establishmentarian. Cultural leaders should frankly face the fact that theism is
dead, they say, and abandon it as a cultural shaping force as soon
as feasible.

The establishmentarian aspirations of such anti-theistic secularists were, however, heady thinking based on the plausible
illusion of an imminent and total secularist triumph. In the 1930s
it looked as though it might be around the corner. As we have
seen, secularists had made huge gains in the preceding fifty years.
Moreover, according to positivist theory of cultural evolution,
the continuation of such gains was inevitable. The advance of
scientific culture seemed irreversible. According to this view, the
intellectual contests between science and traditional religion were
mismatches. All that was needed was proper dissemination of the
more advanced views into backward areas that, for sociological
reasons, had resisted them. One finds these assumptions repeatedly in the confident predictions of the era that fundamentalism
would soon pass away. Nor were such assumptions confined just
to the nontheists. They are also apparent in the writings of so
pious an analyst of fundamentalism as H. Richard Niebuhr,[12] and
they were held in varying degrees by almost all modernist and
moderate theists. It may have been the case that theists outnum-
bered non-theistic secularists even among intellectuals, but the
rules of the academic enterprise were now set to preclude religious talk outside explicitly religious or theological contexts. The
recently dominant Protestants abandoned virtually all of their
academic institutions except theological seminaries. The media
also had secularized. So all in all there seemed to be few serious
challenges facing the secularists' establishmentarian illusions.

Although nontheistic secularists have not given up the fight,
and they still have some important forces of modernization on
their side, World War II struck a serious blow at their establishmentarian dreams in America. The spectacle of Nazism made
many people, including intellectuals, ask what the genius of Western civilization was that could keep it from lapsing into sheer
barbarism. The scientific method plus trust in humanity alone
now seemed, for many, a hollow promise. A wide (though seldom
deep) religious revival began that continues today, though it has

---

12. See Niebuhr's article on fundamentalism in the *Encyclopedia
of Social Sciences* (New York, 1937), 6: 526-27.

passed through several stages since the 1940s.[13] By now the religious revival has gone on long enough and has taken such an unexpected form with the recent resurgence of fundamentalism in America and elsewhere that one of the most basic premises of the positivist evolution-of-culture worldview has been challenged. Perhaps the advance of the positivist scientific worldview, with its corollaries of blind faith in human freedom, is not inevitable and irreversible.

The nontheistic secularists are not inclined to view these developments as a fatal blow to the fundamental premise of their worldview. They consider the current religious revivals temporary, though potentially very dangerous, setbacks. Scientific and humanistic advances may trigger irrational backlashes, they say, pointing to fascism and fundamentalism around the world as evidence. And they warn that these irrational forces could well crush humanity: ignorance could triumph over intelligence and destroy the world with the very techniques and weapons that intelligence has created.

This brings us to the other side of nontheistic secularism, just as important as its establishmentarism. Nontheistic secularists see themselves as a minority sect, threatened with repression and discrimination at the hands of Christian establishmentarians. That is to say that whereas in some contexts they regard themselves as insiders, the proper spokespersons and mentors for all right-thinking Americans, in other contexts they regard themselves as outsiders, threatened by a kind of Christian Americanism that they find alien and dangerous. This latter mood, though not confined to nontheists, was especially apparent during the 1984 election campaign, when there was deep alarm over what Norman Lear called "the Evangelist-in-Chief's ultrafundamentalist theology.[14] Whether or not we think such alarm is justified,

---

13. See C. T. McIntire's *God, History, and Historians: Modern Christian Views of History* (New York: Oxford, 1977) for some of this postwar discussion of the importance of religion to civilization. One sign of the times was that in 1948 Kenneth Scott Latourelle, president of the American Historical Association, gave a presidential address entitled "The Christian Understanding of History" (see the *American Historical Review* 54 [January 1949]: 259-76).

14. Lear, in an open letter from People for the American Way dated October 1984.

it is deeply engraved in the nontheistic secularists' psyche. It is connected with long-standing fears of fascism, nazism, communism, and some of the activities of the American religious right. Historian Leo Ribuffo has referred to these reactions and over-reactions in the 1930s and 1940s as "the Brown Scare."[15]

That nontheistic secularists and their religiously liberal allies should simultaneously hold these two views of their role in America—that of establishmentarian and the threatened sectarian—should not be thought too incongruous or disingenuous. Their stance closely parallels that of American fundamentalists, who are best understood if seen as wavering between the pole of the outsider seeking to flee this world and that of the establishmentarian wanting to take over the world. Indeed, this tension is found throughout Christian history, so it should not be surprising that post-Christian secularists should share it.

Once we understand that the "religious humanism" of nontheistic secularists shares with most branches of Christianity an ambivalence concerning whether to flee from the dominant culture or to control it, we can make some sense of some of their activities. Religions that regard themselves as minorities are likely to champion pluralism and tolerance, and nontheistic secularists have similarly been among this nation's most vocal champions of pluralism. People for the American Way is not made up exclusively of nontheists, although we can assume a substantial nontheist contingent, and it emphasizes that "the alternative to a Christian nation is not a godless America but an America that cherishes a rich diversity of religious and other beliefs among its citizens."[16] Likewise, the American Civil Liberties Union has demonstrated in its defenses of the rights of Jehovah's Witnesses, Seventh-day Adventists, and practicing Jews that it does not oppose the free practice of religion as such.[17] Nonetheless, in the case of the ACLU there is a very clear pattern in the types of

---

15. Ribuffo, *The Old Christian Right: The Protestant Far Right from the Great Depression to the Cold War* (Philadelphia: Temple University Press, 1983).

16. So says Lear in the open letter from People for the American Way.

17. See *The Noblest Cry: A History of the American Civil Liberties Union* (New York: St. Martin's Press, 1965), pp. 132-47.

religious rights causes they champion. Almost invariably, they are defending citizens against the special privileges that still remain from the informal establishment of Christianity in America.[18] Their fears of this establishment may by this time seem excessive and irrational, but we Christians might better empathize with them if we imagined ourselves living in a recently Mormon or Islamic state. Moreover, Jews, who provide a substantial amount of support for the ACLU, have good reasons to fear revivals of Christian civilizations. Certainly their experience encourages the outsider mentality of some anti-theistic secularists.

The maddening tangle of inconsistencies in church and state cases over the past forty years can be explained in part by the insider/outsider, establishmentarian/sectarian, ambivalence of the most vocal defenders of separation. As George Goldberg has recently pointed out, champions of separation say that they are interested in pluralism, and yet they almost always work for eliminating all public religious practices, and almost never work for ensuring equitable public encouragement of all religions and beliefs represented in a community.[19] In part this reluctance is due to the difficulty of giving comparable treatment to organized religion and to unorganized nontheistic faiths, and in part it is due to sectarian fear that in many American communities pressures favoring Christianity would give it an unfair advantage in attempts at public equity. The Voltaire club will not compete well with the Bible club. Clearly, however, there is more than just sectarian fears, even though they are genuine. There is also establishmentarian zeal to get rid of religion, which nontheistic secularists see as damaging to humanity. As one ACLU publication has put it, "Man in general needs myths to try to pretend the truth out of existence, and he will never tolerate those who, having outgrown the need for both myth and crutch, set thus a frightening and humiliating example to their fellows."[20] Both

---

18. See Leo Pfeffer, "The Right to Religious Liberty," in *The Rights of Americans: What They Are—What They Should Be,* ed. Norman Dorsen (New York: Pantheon Books, 1970), pp. 326-47.

19. Goldberg, *Reconsecrating America* (Grand Rapids: Eerdmans, 1984).

20. *The Noblest Cry,* p. 133.

sectarian and establishmentarian tendencies are found in that sentence: we must defend pluralistic rights against religious intolerance, but clearly the larger goal should be to get rid of the crutch.

So what should our attitude be toward nontheistic secularists?

1. We should recognize that they are not a well-organized conspiracy but a disparate group of individuals who happen to hold a set of similar values derived from a long-standing faith in positivism and/or humanist freedom and creativity. Nontheistic secularists appear to have disproportionate influence because some processes of modernization and pluralization speed the secularization of some areas of society and because many theists have conceded that positivist assumptions are the best guides for conducting many human activities.

2. In our dealings with nontheistic secularists we should insist on a careful distinction between their legitimate interests as one of the considerable minorities in American society on the one hand and their establishmentarian aspirations and assumptions on the other. With respect to the former, we can find considerable common ground and common interest in protecting a genuinely pluralistic society. Such recognition of some commonality will enhance the credibility of our adamant resistance to efforts to discriminate against our religious practice, to the extent that it is genuinely pluralistic.

3. To this end, we should avoid pushing for programs that suggest the old establishmentarianism, since these sorts of efforts simply play into the hands of the establishmentarian secularists. Nontheistic secularists and their allies in minority religious groups, especially Jews, can point to a long record of Christians (especially Protestants) having used the state to promote their own religious interests at the expense of the interests of minorities. The nineteenth-century practice of having Protestant worship and teaching essentially Protestant doctrine in public schools is a good example. Advocating policies that smack of such establishmentarianism simply reopens old wounds. Organized school prayers, unless they are made pluralistic and vacuous to the point of being sacrilegious, fall into this category. More clearly counterproductive are misguided efforts such as the attempt to pass laws requiring the teaching of "creation science" (i.e., the contention that the earth is only a few thousand years old and geological

evidence to the contrary can be explained by a worldwide flood) to try to "balance" the secularistic naturalism of much evolutionary science. Even most Christians are discriminated against by such fundamentalistic establishmentarian efforts. Such campaigns simply fuel secularists' fires.

Serious problems remain, however, because partisan nontheistic assumptions are already established in the way most of the subjects are taught in the state schools. This establishment is the result of both the secularist positivist revolution that took place in the universities and elsewhere around a century ago and the myth promoted by some anti-theistic secularists that any talk of religion is illicit. Whatever the causes, the results are sometimes extraordinary. For instance, grade-school American history texts give the impression that religion virtually ceased to exist after the Puritans. Immigrants are mentioned, but their Catholicism is not. Abolitionists are mentioned, but their religious motives are not. The revivals, which Perry Miller said constituted "the dominant theme in America from 1800-1860" are not mentioned.[21] Such empty-headed omissions could be corrected, but in some fields, such as the social sciences, antireligious assumptions are so deeply ingrained in the very definitions of the subjects that they would not so easily be repaired. Moreover, there are sometimes insurmountable problems in trying to represent one outlook fairly without offending the proponents of an alternate viewpoint. For instance, pious advocates of gay rights or women's rights might be offended by accounts written by the equally pious opposition to these stances, and vice versa.

In the particular case of state schools in which pluralism seems to favor nontheism, the obvious solution is to produce a pluralistic school system by using tax dollars to support schools representing a variety of religious and ideological positions.[22]

---

21. See Robert Bryan's pamphlet "History, Pseudo-History, Anti-History: How Public-School Textbooks Treat Religion" (Washington: Learn, 1983).

22. For an elaboration of this argument, see Rockne N. McCarthy, James W. Skillen, and William A. Harper, *Disestablishment a Second Time: Genuine Pluralism for American Schools* (Grand Rapids: Eerdmans, 1982).

At this point, however, we should broaden our focus from the alleged threat of nontheistic secularists to the broader questions of secularization and attempt to find some general principles that will help us deal with them.

To do so, we should first briefly take into account the role of theistic secularists or secularizers, who may well constitute a larger group than the nontheists. Theistic secularizers are spread across a broad spectrum of viewpoints, of course. Many who are conservative in their religious professions unwittingly contribute to secularization by giving religious sanction to worldly practices or by so narrowly confining their piety as not to relate it to much else that they do. Other theists—probably most of us—would favor carefully selective secularization of public life as a means of promoting equity and public tranquility.

Still another prominent group of theistic secularizers demands a bit more attention. The religious liberals who tend to ally themselves with nontheistic secularists on almost all the issues we have been discussing constitute another "elite" that has on the whole abetted the secularization of society. We might be tempted to wonder why such groups as the National Council of Churches are apparently working to put themselves out of business. Their actions are understandable given a few of their premises, however. First of all, they recognize and take seriously some of the real problems of maintaining justice for all religious groups in a pluralistic society. Moreover, mainline Protestants recognize that their progenitors have in the past done the most to compromise equal treatment of all religious groups, and they are commendably eager to correct some of those abuses. To this end they are willing to regard themselves as one sect in a pluralistic society. On the other hand, like most of the rest of us, they have establishmentarian aspirations as well. These must be understood in terms of some of their prevailing assumptions about what Christianity is (not all such religious groups hold to these specific assumptions, but they do seem to prevail in practice). They are that Christianity is essentially a divinely sanctioned, progressive-liberal ethical system and that its goals are best realized by infusing the society with progressive-liberal values. Tolerance of diversity is very high on this ethical scale. The only enemies are those who hold religious or other ideologies that are exclusivist or intolerant. Moreover, such values as accepting others and encouraging God's people to treat one another as brothers and sisters fit well with the version of humanistic values that has prevailed in twentieth-century American public life. Such a value system is not especially threatened by there being large areas of public activity where direct reference to theism is eliminated. As long as a progressive-liberal ethical system of nonjudgmental openness and tolerance prevails, secularism seems no great threat. In practical terms, the progressive-liberal contingent makes theism secondary to maintaining these moral values in the culture and places political programs based on moral principles among their chief means for promoting the kingdom.

This brings us to the much-debated issue of religion and politics. In his valuable and provocative book *The Naked Public Square*, Richard Neuhaus has suggested that the crisis in American public life should be understood as a crisis in public moral philosophy. We are in danger, he says, of allowing a religious-moral vacuum at the center of our culture that will be an invitation to totalitarianism. This analysis, however, for all its insights, misconceives the issue at a crucial point. Neuhaus's whole analysis is built on the premise that "religion is the morality-bearing part of culture."[23] The problem as he describes it, then, is that religion is receding from public life (broadly conceived), leaving a moral vacuum, and the solution must be to put more religion back into the public square.

This premise, however, is mistaken. Although theistic religion is one of the morality-bearing parts of our culture, it certainly is not the only one. Nontheistic secularism also promotes a morality. The problem is not simply whether or not we have morality in public life; more basically, it is that we have competing moral systems and hence less of a consensus in public philosophy than we might like. Putting more religion into public life will not resolve this problem, unless we first decide whose religion it will be. And since there is even less consensus regarding religion than there is regarding public philosophy, it is difficult to see how adding more religion would move us toward the needed consensus. As we have already noted, mainline Protestantism tends to

---

23. Neuhaus, *The Naked Public Square* (Grand Rapids: Eerdmans, 1984), p. 154.

support a moral system similar to that advocated by nontheistic secularists, so having more Presbyterian, Methodist, or United Church of Christ religion in the public square will not produce the moral consensus that Neuhaus desires.

Moreover, those who want both to put more religion into the public square and to maintain its civility are faced with another major difficulty. How are moderates such as Neuhaus and the "elite" that he hopes will shape the moral consensus going to control the ideologues of the right or the left? The fact is that religion and power is a very volatile mix. If one combines the ability to force one's will on others with the absolute religious conviction that one is right, the chances of tyranny, or civil warfare are vastly increased. Religious convictions can all too easily become a sort of wild card that one puts together with whatever political bias one happens to hold. When such combinations are encouraged, the chances are magnified of disastrous showdowns between two parties, each claiming unbeatable hands. Northern Ireland, Lebanon, and Iran are all notable examples of the dangers of religion in the public square. So more religion may not be as helpful a response to more public secularity as it may seem at first.

Not only is the simple increase in religion not self-evidently beneficial for public life, but from the point of view of the serious Christian it may pose a threat to the more important cause of the kingdom. If we use "secularity" in a normative context to refer to the decline or retreat of true religion, then it should be evident that secularity can increase even as religious (or even "Christian") profession and practice increases. For instance, if Christians simply baptize worldly practice (e.g., pure self-interest or materialism), the resultant increase in the popularity of Christianity will not retard the growth of true secularity. Most religious commentators on secularization, however, confuse the descriptive use of secularization with this normative sense. Hence, reports that America's origins were especially religious or "Christian" usually miss the point.[24]

A supressed Constantinianism is often present in Christian

---

24. For more on this, see Mark A. Noll, Nathan O. Hatch, and George M. Marsden, *The Search for Christian America* (Westchester, Ill.: Crossway Books, 1983).

commentary on secularization in normative contexts. Such discussions often start by assuming medieval or Reformation establishmentarian standards and then describe almost everything that has occurred since as though it were, normatively speaking, a decline. The picture, however, would look different if we used as our normative standard the pre-Constantinian ancient church. Then we would see much more clearly that the decline of public and professed Christianity (to say nothing of "religion") is a much more mixed story, normatively speaking.

Having said all this, I would now like to return to the political side of the discussion to suggest that we can learn something from the American tradition in addition to simply glorying in its religiosity.

As I have observed elsewhere in commenting on this subject, when I went back to my hometown in central Pennsylvania last summer to sell our century-and-a-half-old family home, I was struck with the apparent intent of the eighteenth-century founders of the town to keep religion out of the public square. In a departure from the common practice throughout Christendom, lots for churches were deeded to the Moravians, the Presbyterians, and the Lutherans when the town was laid out, but not on the public square. Eighteenth-century Pennsylvania was justly celebrated as a model of religious liberty, and I think we can learn something from the principle that the town founders appear to have followed. Of course the physical separation is not in itself the crucial point; the point is, contra Neuhaus, that the naked public square could be a symbol of what is *right* about the American tradition rather than of what is wrong. In my hometown, religion was encouraged, but it was *distanced* from the public square. Since the town planners actually encouraged the founding of churches, this distancing cannot be interpreted as advocacy of a "wall of separation" between church and state. Nor would such distancing do much to keep religious groups from contributing to the discourse concerning public moral philosophy. It would simply force them to translate their recommendations into terms that did not appeal solely to principles peculiar to their sect.[25]

---

25. Neuhaus favors this latter point; see *The Naked Public Square,* p. 36.

*   *   *

These observations regarding one's stance toward secularization in politics point to some general principles that seriously religious people might hold in dealing with the secularization of American society and with those, both theists and nontheists, who advocate further secularization.

First of all, we misconceive the problem if we think of it as basically a confrontation between the positive value of religion and the negative value of secularization. Nor is it the reverse. The situation is more complicated and calls for a delicate balance between the interests of religions and the forces of secularization. It is for this reason that I propose distancing religion from the public square as a worthwhile working principle. This approach has the advantage of sharing some of the interests of the non-theistic secularists and hence perhaps providing a basis for working out a *modus vivendi*. If such distancing is a firm part of our public philosophy, it also helps protect us from something any serious religious believer should be concerned about—the takeover of the public square by a false religion. At the same time, however, such distancing would allow us to cherish the constitutional principle of encouraging all religions and inviting them all to participate civilly in shaping public moral philosophy.

Behind this principle of distancing is another principle just as basic for this analysis—the distinction between secularization as a proper methodology/technique and secularism as a worldview. Most of natural science and technology involves the use of a secularized methodology that entails temporarily excluding religious and spiritual considerations for the purposes of analyzing natural causes. It should be strongly emphasized, however, that such methodologies are artificial and do not themselves constitute worldviews. The same principle should apply to civic affairs. In courts of law we all accept a methodology that excludes almost all religious or spiritual considerations as evidence in a case. Nonetheless, we should emphasize that this technique, helpful for promoting judicial equity, does not constitute a worldview. Nor does it imply that we can or should remove ethical considerations from our concepts of law. Similarly, for purposes of civil tranquility and justice in a multireligious society, it may be necessary to distance most religious considerations from government activities, though we cannot and should not remove ethical considerations. Similarly, in the social sciences and history, distancing ourselves from our religious commitments may serve as a legitimate technique for some limited purposes such as for empathizing with our subjects or for communicating with a wider audience. But such distancing should not involve abandoning considerations of morality (though we might do well to withhold our judgments for a time). Nor should such distancing be mistaken for anything like an adequate basis for a worldview.

This distinction between technique and worldview is especially valuable in addressing the anti-theistic secularist. Such secularists present the proven efficacy of secularized or positivist techniques as powerful arguments for nontheistic worldviews. With our distinction in mind, however, we can grant them the value of such techniques in their proper place and at the same time insist that nothing in those techniques entails the superiority of a nontheistic worldview. In fact, some of the widely recognized problems of civilizations built largely on such techniques might argue well for looking outside the material world for the basis of a worldview. But that is another story.

From Providence to Privacy: Religion and the Redefinition of America

Richard John Neuhaus

Defining and redefining America is a very American thing to be doing. "American history does not explain itself," the late Sydney Ahlstrom was fond of saying. This may be the case with any nation's history, but in the case of America it is more so. America is, as many historians have noted, an experiment. John Courtney Murray spoke of "the American proposition," which, if it is to endure, must ever be reproposed. Most majestically, Lincoln understood America as "a new nation, conceived in Liberty, and dedicated to the proposition that all men are created equal."

It might be objected that we should let the thus-and-so-ness, the sheer facticity, of America speak for itself. But it is precisely respect for facticity that engages us in the definitional enterprise, for an inescapable fact about America and Americans is our propensity to define and redefine ourselves. In other words, that America is ever defining itself is an essential part of the definition of America. America is not a fact of nature but a product of human decision. It is a nation on purpose and by purpose. As with any decision, it requires explanation and justification. Just as we have all decided to participate in a conference on religion in American life and can therefore ask what we are here for, so the Americans can and do ask of themselves "What are we here for?"

Of course not all Americans ask that question, and those who do ask it, do not all ask it in the same way or with the same

52

degree of urgency. But thoughtful people (that is to say, people who ask such questions) seek not only explanation but justification of the American reality. Justification means (also and perhaps preeminently) moral justification. Nationhood itself requires justification. The idea of nation entails power, breadth, permanence, and claims to majesty that are not self-evidently justified. All nations attempt to give an answer to the question of what they are there for. But in most other nations the question is not asked with such urgency, either by its own people or by others. The "thereness" of America, however, looms so large, impinges so massively upon the world-historical scene that even if we wanted to evade the question of what we are here for, the rest of the world would not let us.

We should not want to evade the question. One reason that some of us try to evade it is that we have lost confidence in the old answers that were given to the question. Paul Johnson's paper reminds us what some of those answers were, and to many of our cultural elite they sound embarrassingly antique. Who today, apart from some politicians on ritual occasions, says that America is embarked upon a providentially guided errand into the wilderness? Lincoln declared that "we shall nobly save, or meanly lose, the last, best hope of earth." What is lost today—meanly or otherwise—is the belief that America is in any way the bearer of a universal hope.

Many causes can be cited, and are cited, to explain why we have lost confidence in the old answers. I suggest that a causal factor, maybe the major causal factor, is that the old answers are unabashedly moral. It is a dogma of our high culture that it is morally required to reject morally normative assertions as dogmatism. Not only are the old answers moral, but they are lethally tainted by religious belief. And America is, as we all presumably know, a secular society. Embarrassed by the old answers, and bereft of new answers, we determine to get along without answers.

Or, put differently, we say that the answer is the success of what America manifestly is. Ted Morgan (On Becoming American) has remarked that America is a success by the same measure that a Broadway play is a success: people are lined up around the block trying to get in. Our formidable economic successes, our political stability, our globe-sprawling military power, our world-shaping cultural exports—this is what America is, and what Amer-

ica is is what America is for. Those who take consolation from
this tautology overlook some critical facts, I believe. This puta-
tive definition of America is perilously contingent upon sustained
success. It will not sustain us in the trials of failure, and a national
purpose that cannot make sense of sacrifice in times of trial is no
national purpose at all.

Moreover, as Reinhold Niebuhr wrote in 1952 (*The Irony
of American History*), this approach fails to take account of the
fact that in the view of our opponents it is precisely our success
that damns us. They measure our success in terms of our enthrall-
ing the youth of the world with punk rock and blue jeans. With
greater moral urgency and political consequence, they take our
success to be the explanation of the world's failure, notably the
failure of "the poor and oppressed of the Third World." Of
course Niebuhr assumed that America had ideologically committed and aggressive opponents, an assumption not shared today by
many Americans who get paid to think. But opponents there are,
and they have an explanation for the world's suffering: the facts
about America's success are too good to be good.

The facts of America, then, will not provide a definition of
America.

People—all people, we may assume—are meaning-asking
and meaning-making creatures. Not only three-year-old children
but all of us persist in asking Why. Why should I do this? Because it is in the national interest. Why should I care about the
national interest? Because ... and we become stumbling and
tongue-tied. Some evangelicals and fundamentalists have an answer: Because America is God's launching pad for the evan-
gelization of the world in preparation for the End Time. But that
is not a culturally respectable answer. It is not even—not even
nearly—as respectable as the older American answers by which
we are also embarrassed. The culturally respectable answers (if
any answers are to be suggested at all) usually come down to
something about the national interest being in our self-interest.
And then, because people want to make not only meanings but
moral meanings, there may follow some speculation about whether
our interests will, in the long run, serve the interests of others as
well. But the utilities of utilitarianism, whether vulgar or sophisticated, are so very iffy. Then too, in the long run, as it is fashion-
ably said, we are all dead. Meanwhile, there are people explaining
in ways that many find plausible why America's interests are

against the interests of the world, especially the world of the most pitiable and morally compelling. The "preferential option for the poor" is of necessity, they say, a preferential option against the rich. Or, as a presidential candidate recently put it, "America is on the wrong side of the world revolution."

In the absence of a morally explicit and morally convincing answer to the question of what America is for, it is hard either to affirm or to criticize what America is. We cannot do without a defined self-understanding. With respect to both our domestic life and our role in the world, criticism of what we are presupposes a measure of agreement on what we are supposed to be. Our adversaries, who truly believe or are tragically stuck with interpreting reality by their historical dialectic, think they know how *the world* is supposed to be. And they are sure they know how America is (temporarily) preventing the world from becoming what it is supposed to be and will inevitably become. It is difficult to counter their idea with a non-idea. Yet the non-idea about America is what many of us have in principle pledged ourselves to. Boasting of our deficiency, we take pride in being non-ideological. Ideology, however, is, in its first meaning, nothing more than a systematic and coordinated set of ideas in support of a social or political purpose. It is curious that we deem it a virtue to have unsystematic and uncoordinated ideas. Or perhaps the virtue is in having no ideas. Most likely, the presumed virtue is in having no purpose.

It may be argued that this is an instance of making a virtue of necessity. The necessity is to recognize that the old statements of national purpose are no longer plausible; or, if they are plausible, they are no longer safe. We once asked how to make the world safe for democracy, for example. Now the question is how to make the world safe *from* democracy, or at least from anything that Americans might recognize as democracy. The necessity, we are told, derives from the fact that America has lost its innocence, and none too soon. To paraphrase Nixon on Keynes, we are all postlapsarians now. A decade and more ago, some theologians told us that we are "man come of age" and this necessarily entails the "death of God." So now some tell us that we are a nation come of age, and this necessarily entails the death of the American Dream. Grown-ups, my dear, don't keep on asking Why.

If America is for nothing in particular, I have suggested that we are ideationally outgunned by our adversaries. I do not wish to dwell excessively on the external threat, however, lest I be taken for a cold warrior or, God forbid, an anti-Communist. Also in our domestic life, the meaning of politics is morally eviscerated. Without answers to our *Why*, politics ceases to be a moral enterprise in the way that John Winthrop or Thomas Jefferson or, for that matter, Aristotle understood politics to be a moral enterprise. Then we are reduced to what Theodore Lowi calls "interest group liberalism." It is a liberalism that, by libertarian translation, can also pass as conservatism. And the "interest" in question is usually thought to be an economic interest. The problem with the interpretation of America that we receive in the press and on television is not, as some say, that it is excessively politicized. It is that politics has been, so to speak, economized. We all know, do we not, that elections and almost everything else turn on "the pocketbook issues."

In the great tradition, the great question of politics is how we are to live together. It is an inescapably moral question. Aristotle's *Politics* and his *Ethics* are, by his own acknowledgment, one study. In the American tradition, the response to the great question has traditionally involved a purpose to which we are pledged and a promise in which we believe. Individual Americans may still affirm such purposes and promises privately, and, as noted earlier, public officials may do so publicly on a few ceremonial occasions. But in prestige discourse about public matters, in discourse approved by the canons of academe, references to purpose and promise, if they occur at all, are qualified by quotation marks. That is required, according to some, because such references are to "values" (which are private) rather than to "facts" (which are public). And there are those who do not subscribe to such a sharp dichotomy between value and fact and yet still do not find the old values very persuasive. Even if we agreed on the need for publicly asserted purpose and promise, we would still have to agree on *what* purpose and *what* promise. Therefore, it is argued, such assertions are "divisive" and violate the rules of a "pluralistic society." Those who argue this way, I suggest, do not understand the meaning of pluralism. What they call pluralism is in reality the public monism of studied indifference to the visions of purpose and promise professed by the people of this democratic society.

Our most popularly rooted sense of purpose is that we ought to be a democratic society. The democratic idea means, inter alia, that it is the national purpose to sustain and protect the many purposes of persons and persons-in-community. In shortest form, the idea is freedom. (There is a long-standing debate about whether equality should be given equal billing with freedom, but I will not get into that here except to say that in the American proposal equality serves freedom, and the two should not be viewed as antagonists.) The assertion of democratic purpose is surrounded by the aura of the promise that ours is not an idiosyncratic or purely self-interested experiment. It suggests that what we are doing has world-historical significance, that it somehow portends a future of freedom and that, as a promise, it is still awaiting definitive vindication "under God."

Do I say that this is the way most Americans talk about national purpose and promise? Of course not. But until the past several decades those who talked about national purpose and promise did so in this fashion. These are the intuitions that are still popularly and deeply rooted in American life. These are the "mystic chords" that are struck to powerful effect by artful politicians still today. And these are the intuitions, beliefs, and assertions that are, with few exceptions, declared inadmissible in culturally elite arenas of public discourse. Of course they may be discussed under the rubric of folk superstitions. Their existence is acknowledged in order to explain why certain politicians are able to exploit nostalgia for a remembered past which, we are quick to add, never really was. Thus is intellectual discourse about the democratic idea safely insulated from the democratic reality of the American people.

The problematic connections between the democratic idea and religion (and religiously grounded values) has, of course, a long history. We have indeed come a long way from the situation described by historian Edward Purcell:

> During the nineteenth century Americans had generally accepted the validity of democratic government with neither qualms nor qualifications. The democratic ideal was the unquestioned American ideal, and it was widely accepted as an axiom of life. Though Americans were unconcerned with elaborate theoretical justifications, they were nevertheless convinced that democracy was both rationally and morally the best possible form of government. Religious faith, national tradition, a moderate rationalism going back to the ideas of the Declaration of Independence, and

the concrete experience of most Americans all testified to the validity and certainty of its ideals.*

Enter, early in this century, the nontheistic secularizers of George Marsden's paper, who were frequently and passionately anti-theistic. In some cases, new ideas running under the banner of empiricism and evolution were melded into the old ideas supportive of the democratic idea. This was notably the case in the work of such leaders as James and Dewey. But there were also more aggressive efforts that rejected the possibility of demonstrating the truth of ethical propositions by either induction or deduction, thus leaving moral ideas, including the democratic idea, without a rational theoretical foundation. In 1925 Albert Paul Weiss declared that the science of behaviorism "assumes that man's educational, vocational and social activities can be completely described or explained as the result of the same (and no other) forces used in the natural sciences." "What we need," wrote Luther L. Bernard in the same period, "is objectively tested fact to replace our venerable traditions." Famed mathematician Eric Temple Bell asserted that "the philosophic theory of values is to the propagation of bunk what a damp, poorly lighted cellar is to that of mushrooms." "To state the matter bluntly," Bell wrote, "the supreme importance of the Greece of Aristotle, Plato, and Euclid for the history of abstract thinking is this: in that Golden Age were forged the chains with which human reason was bound for 2300 years." In anthropology, the students of the great Boas, including Margaret Mead, asserted that all values can be graded only on subjective and "culturally conditioned" grounds and are therefore incommensurable. The result is "the impossibility of grading cultures." Given that impossibility, it is a preposterous arrogance to affirm the superiority, never mind the universal validity, of the democratic idea.

An elite consensus formed that only an absolute relativity absolutely opposed to absolutes is compatible with the cherished, albeit relative, values of democracy. As the totalitarian clouds gathered—Bolshevik, Italian Fascist, Nazi—a counterview began to gain a hearing. Mortimer Adler and Robert Hutchins at the

---

* Purcell, *The Crisis of Democratic Theory: Scientific Naturalism and the Problem of Value* (Lexington: University Press of Kentucky, 1973), p. 5. The several illustrations following are also drawn from this very useful study in the history of ideas.

University of Chicago were in the lead of those contending that only transcendent truth of a metaphysical if not theological nature could support the democratic proposition. Hutchins set forth five logically related ideas in which we "must believe" if we are to justify democracy: (1) that human beings act not from instinct alone but through the power of reason, (2) that nonempirical truth exists, (3) that an objective ethical standard exists, (4) that the proper end of humanity is the fulfillment of our moral and intellectual powers, and (5) that all these truths can be known explicitly through the process of right reason. "If we do not believe in this basis of this end," Hutchins concluded, "we do not believe in democracy."

In religious thought, of course, the counterattack was led by the prodigiously productive Reinhold Niebuhr. In 1940 he joined with Lewis Mumford, Van Wyck Brooks, Hans Kohn, and others in issuing "A Declaration on World Democracy." "War, declared or undeclared, actual or virtual, has chosen us," they announced, and America was unprepared because it had been the victim of "an education adrift in a relativity that doubted all values, and a degraded science that shirked the spiritual issues." They concluded that "this recognition of guilt [by intellectuals] must pave the way, not to maudlin regrets, but to immediate atonement." Atonement, immediate or otherwise, was not forthcoming, but during the years of World War II, intellectuals generally did their part in publicly affirming that democracy is inseparable from the values of Western civilization, including (although many hedged on this) Judeo-Christian religion. Unlike another president who said much the same thing in 1984, President Roosevelt was not derided when in 1939 he told Congress that religion is "the source" of democracy: "Religion, by teaching man his relationship to God, gives an individual a sense of his own dignity and teaches him to respect himself by respecting his neighbors."

According to Purcell's account, the counterattack quickly fizzled out with the ending of the war. The radical relativists—or, as he calls them, the "scientific naturalists"—were once again in the driver's seat, and metaphysics, not to mention religion, was definitely not invited to go along. In Purcell's view, even Reinhold Niebuhr had joined the camp of the radical relativists. His defense of democracy, says Purcell, rests upon what is little more than a biblical version of William James's "open universe." Permit me to note, as an aside, that I believe Purcell, along with others, misreads Niebuhr on this score. True, Niebuhr saw himself as a Jamesian, which in my view is neither a moral nor an intellectual fault. But, far from trimming biblical truth to relativist fashion, Niebuhr's teaching regarding the radical nature of evil and the provisional nature of our historical moment has ample basis in historic Christian doctrine. Today, it is worth noting, most liberal Protestant thinkers, to the extent they deal with Niebuhr at all, deem him impossibly absolutistic and consider his religiously grounded argument for democracy to be dangerously conducive to "cold-warrism."

In any event, our intellectual situation today is strikingly similar to that which prevailed from the second decade of this century up through the mid-1930s, when it was temporarily changed by the undeniable external threat of totalitarianism. Today most intellectuals find the threat of totalitarianism eminently deniable. Yet there are strong and, I believe, building counterforces to the prevailing intellectual style. These forces are intellectual, political, and religious. In combination they may portend a profound cultural shift in our understanding of America and the democratic idea it is for. Our present moment and the decades ahead, it is reasonable to think, may best be described as a *Kulturkampf* over the defining of the American experiment.

Intellectually, what is now called neoconservatism not only represents disillusionment with earlier liberal policies but in many cases stands as a challenge to reigning assumptions of the secular Enlightenment, including the exclusion of moral, metaphysical, and religious vision from the public arena. Politically, what is taken to be a conservative tide is driven in large part by a populist protest against the undemocratic imposition of a secular and secularizing definition of American life. What are called "the social issues" are deeper and more important, I believe, than the pundits of interest-group liberalism can allow or some survey research data indicate. Prominent in this protest is what is called the religious new right, but it is by no means alone. The movement also includes less populist, more culturally secure Americans of every religious faith and none.

The movement is sometimes called "traditionalist" or the "back-to-basics movement." But that is to define it much too narrowly, in terms that register specific "issues" on the political screen of today and tomorrow. The movement is in large part a

mood, the protest in large part an uneasiness—about the public
loss of transcendence, about a perceived moral vacuum at the
heart of our public life, about the absence of a sense of interest-
surpassing content and consequence in the American enterprise.
This uneasiness is not limited to America. It was reflected by the
late Kenneth Clark toward the end of his famed television series
"Civilisation." "For a thousand years, civilisation was Christian
civilisation," he says. And then, with an air of puzzlement, he
observes that seemingly all of a sudden we stopped calling it that
and said it had nothing to do with us. His implication was that
this is the only civilization we have; we cannot cut ourselves
loose from it and still be civilized.

If we do cut ourselves loose from the past, the result will
not be, as some suggest, a new paganism. Pagan culture, after all,
is possessed of a certain nobility. As C. S. Lewis reminded us, "a
post-Christian man is not a pagan; you might as well think that
a married woman recovers her virginity by divorce. The post-
Christian is cut off from the Christian past and therefore doubly
from the pagan past." Alasdair MacIntyre surely has it right
when he says that the world that has come "after virtue" is not
pagan but barbarian, and the barbarians "have already been gov-
erning us for quite some time now." Unlike MacIntyre, I find a
measure of encouragement in the challenges now being raised to
the rule of the barbarians.

The scientific reductionism that is now being challenged is
not only hostile to religion, especially religion in public. It is also
devoted to a radical process of removing cultural and historical
referents from our common life. Because religion is, I believe, at
the heart of culture, it is only the most egregious offender against
this worldview, which asserts itself at all levels of American life.
In an intellectually elegant form, it is the spirit that moves John
Rawls's anonymous, deracinated, dehistoricized rational beings
defining justice behind a "veil of ignorance." Rawls's hypotheti-
cal exercise in selfishness and ignorance is wrongly criticized as
an example of individualism run amok. Rawls's individuals are
abstracted from all social, historical, and communal particularities, and therefore have no individuality whatsoever, for it is only
in interaction with these communal particularities that the individual can become individual.

The scientific reductionism being protested is evident in
the 1973 Roe v. Wade decision on abortion. Students of law have

observed that in this case, for the first time in American jurisprudence, the Supreme Court explicitly excluded philosophy, ethics, and religion as factors in its deliberation. This raises a most solemn question: Whom do we recognize as members of the community with a claim upon legal protection? The history of the community's reflection upon that question was not admitted behind the court's veil of ignorance. Medical—which is to say technical—evidence was admissible, on the other hand. Knowing that such a decision should nonetheless have the appearance of moral justification, the court searched for some covering "value" and came up with the value of privacy. Much of the course of public reasoning in America can be read from the fact that our highest appeal is no longer to Providence but to privacy.

Illustrations are all too abundant. The New York City public school system is now introducing a curriculum on "Family Living and Sex Education" for kindergarten through grade twelve. Combing through hundreds of pages of the texts being used in this endeavor, one finds no clue that our culture is rich in poetic, literary, musical, philosophical, and religious reflection on the meaning of sex, love, marriage, and family. There is no reference to any sort of tradition; everything begins now and from scratch. The only factors in play are anatomy, the individual's "emotional needs," peer approval, and (very marginally) what is legally permissible. As the instructions to the teacher make clear, even the teacher is not there as teacher but only as facilitator of student "value choices."

Or consider the recent decision of the highest court in the state of New York to remove the "marital exemption" in cases of rape. Anything that discourages wife-abuse is, of course, to be welcomed. Not so welcome is the judicial reasoning that declares it "irrational" and "absurd" to think that in marriage a woman surrenders any of her rights, "including the right to control her own body." It is at least worth asking whether, perhaps in every culture, the key to the meaning of marriage is not the mutual surrender of certain rights, or at least the agreement to limit the exercise of certain rights. Of course a greater degree of mutuality might be desired between husband and wife with respect to such self-limitation, but the court's reasoning is an assault upon communal obligation as such—except, of course, for the obligation of the individual to obey the laws of the state. Most pertinent to our discussion is the fact that the court's opinion recognizes no duty to cultural tradition; indeed, it refers to tradition only in order to dismiss it.

From John Rawls to marital rape. It may seem that the connections are somewhat stretched, but the point is that matters of history and cultural tradition are being drained from our public discourse. In a very important respect, the exclusion of religion from the public arena is part of the exclusion of the culturally normative. What is discretely identifiable as religion is not, of course, the only morality-bearing part of culture. Literature, the arts, and philosophy, as well as business and engineering all bear moral content. There are, therefore, moralities in conflict as well as in complementarity. And there is morality, indeed religion, in the position of those who would exorcise brand-name religion from public discourse and eviscerate politics of its moral character by turning it into the brokering of interests. That this too is a religion, albeit a religion that dare not speak its name, is the truth perceived by those who attack, and too often rail against, "secular humanism."

As it happens, however, the overwhelming majority of Americans identify self-confessed religion as the morality-bearing component in culture. And this does not just "happen" to be the case. They claim to have thought about it and to really believe it. It is a belief that they go to great pains to transmit to their children, which I take to be testimony of their sincerity. They look to religion for the *truth* about the world of which they are part, and about their prospects in the world to come. They look to religion for *help* in numerous ways—spiritual, psychological, material, and social. But—and on this they are almost unanimously agreed—they also look to religion for *morality*. In their view morality is "of course" derived from the Ten Commandments or the Sermon on the Mount or the teaching of the church, even if they are not very familiar with the specific content of any of these.

The assault upon culture is most popularly and passionately protested when it touches upon that part of culture that is identified as religion. The American people do not understand, and I do not think they are going to come to understand, why the Ten Commandments cannot be posted on the schoolroom wall. Of course any thoughtful believer will be at least uneasy about the popularly assumed convergence of religious truth, conventional morality, and the American Way of Life. Of course our immediate concern as believers is not to ask whether religion in America is *true* or *authentic* religion as measured by whatever ultimate norms we adhere to. And of course in my capacity as a theologian I view American religiosity as a mishmash of truth and untruth, authenticity and self-deception that offers a field day for any would-be Kierkegaard eager to expose religious hypocrisies. But that much said, I am nonetheless speaking about the religion of the American people. It is closely related to what Sidney Mead calls "the religion of the republic," and it is inseparable from the popularly recognized meaning of the American experiment.

I return to the point that we need something like an ideology. Perhaps I might better say we need a "common faith" or a "democratic faith." For reasons I have set forth elsewhere, I do not think "civil religion" is the right term. My own preference is for "public philosophy." Whatever it is called, that is what we need. And, thank Nature and Nature's God, that is what we have, and will continue to have if in this *Kulturkampf* we prevail over the views of those who would hide America from itself. We do not have to go behind a veil of ignorance to invent this public philosophy; we have only to insert ourselves into its continuing self-assertion, self-examination, and self-redefinition in the actualities of American life.

Religion is critical to this process, but I agree wholeheartedly with George Marsden that it is best not to have the churches right on the public square. They bear moral meanings that help form the matrix of the discourse in the public square, but the meanings asserted within the walls of the church and the hearts of believers must be *mediated* through public reasoning to play their part in the public square. Public philosophy is the mediating language between religious truth and public decision. The religious new right, generally speaking, does not yet understand this. Typically fundamentalist ideas about the relationship between faith and reason, nature and grace, revelation and history are not designed to contribute to democratic discourse in the manner here proposed. On the whole, fundamentalists do not understand that we cannot make public policy on the basis of private truths. That way lies raw majoritarianism or religious warfare or both.

The remedy for the naked square is not the insertion of naked religion. Religion must be clothed, translated, and interpreted in a mediating language that makes its publicly relevant meanings accessible to all the public. Whatever one may think of the bishops' pronouncements on specific policies, the Roman Catholic tradition is well situated to make such pronouncements. It has, along with some other traditions, consistently asserted that there is no truth pertinent to human governance that is not accessible to human reason. That is among the reasons why I believe that this should be, although quite possibly will not be, "the Catholic moment" in the history of culture-forming religion in America.

If America is to be newly defined by a public philosophy for free society, that definition will be strongly stamped by religion. Already many in our society are uneasy and some profess to be terrified by the reemergence of Religious America. Some are anxious that this means Christian America, and others that it means Fundamentalist Christian America. Yet others, exploiting the not-so-latent anti-Catholicism in American life, especially among intellectuals, raise the alarm of Catholic America. Some who recognize the need for a "moral renewal" hope, as John Dewey hoped, that a moral order can be reasserted apart from, or as a substitute for, troublesome religion. That is not likely to happen, because morality (at least popular morality) must be based on something other than morality. When morality justifies itself by more ultimate truth claims, as it inevitably must, it is recognized by other religions as the religion that it is—and it is then fought, as "secular humanism" is now being fought.

The prospect of Religious America will also be fought, as it is now being fought. It will be fought by some who dissent from brand-name religion itself or from the definition of the American experiment that such religion supports or from both. If the *Kulturkampf* is not to become bloody, it is as important as it is difficult to convince such dissenters that their safety is best secured by the respect for dissenters that is mandated by the common faith from which they dissent.

For reasons both complex and painfully plain, this raises questions of critical importance to the Jewish communities in America. For decades it has been the consensus among Jewish leaders (apart from some of the Orthodox) that the more secular the society the safer it is for Jews and other minorities. Today that consensus is being reexamined and new possibilities are being explored. I hope that reexamination will continue, for I am confident that if the creativity of American Jewry is not engaged in the project, the hoped-for redefinition of America will not succeed.

In summary, then, the defining and redefining of America is a very American thing to do. It is a necessary thing to do for the vitality and perhaps the survival of this experiment in the democratic idea. We have seen that earlier in this century democratic theory faced and survived crisis, however battered. The present discussion of a public philosophy is in many ways at one with the tradition of Lippmann and Dewey. Unlike Lippmann, I argue that that philosophy must serve democratic governance, and, unlike both Lippmann and Dewey, I am convinced that such a philosophy can neither ignore nor replace the religious allegiances of the American people. I have further proposed that the hostility to religion in law, education, and public policy today is part of a larger hostility to normative culture. Indeed, it is hostility to civilization historically defined—and civilization can only be defined historically.

Two final words. First, I am not at all sure that we will succeed in constructing or reconstructing a vibrant public philosophy for this experiment in democratic governance. Second, I am convinced not only by social and historical analysis but as a believer and theologian that Lincoln was probably right: "We shall nobly save, or meanly lose, the last, best hope of earth."

The Story of an Encounter

The twenty-seven people brought together at the Princeton Club in New York City for a conference on "Unsecular America" had more than one thing in common. They all, from whatever discipline, were students of what are called "American values." More specifically, they had a personal and professional interest in how religion shapes the way in which Americans think about, among other things, America. Then too, they were not unsympathetic to the new aggressiveness of religion in the public square—although their levels of sympathy ranged from partisan enthusiasm to wary fascination. Finally, it is fair to say that they shared the bias that there is much that is promising and worth sustaining in the democratic project as Americans have experienced that project. Undoubtedly other commonalities could be discovered in this group. But I think I've said enough to indicate that the gathering was, by design, not necessarily representative of all Americans, nor even of all academics who involve themselves in questions of "religion and society." On the basis of key shared presuppositions, this group intended to sort out its disagreements and explore the further consequences of its agreements.

"Just the facts, ma'am," Sergeant Friday of *Dragnet* used to say. Everett Ladd of The Roper Center, on the other hand, had been asked to summarize the facts and also to present his interpretation. Supplementing his paper and the pertinent data, both of which appear in this volume, Ladd quoted approvingly this conclusion of a recent study by James Reichley of the Brookings Institution.

LADD: Fortunately for the health of American democracy, Americans remain, despite recent incursions by civil humanism and a relentless promotion of egoism, overwhelmingly, in Justice Jackson's words, "a religious people." By all the indices of public opinion surveys, most Americans are religious. For the time being, at least, the commitment of most Americans to a theistic interpretation of existence appears firm. From the beginning of American history, religion and the practice of democracy have been closely intertwined. This relationship, despite changes in structure and recurring tensions, shows no signs of breaking.

While not disputing the facts, some participants thought Ladd's analysis a bit too sanguine. As one party put it, "What you're basically saying is that things are pretty much the same and pretty much the same is OK." Ladd rightly protested this caricature of his presentation but confessed that he is, without apology, very hopeful about the vitalities of religion in American life. Theodore Caplow of the University of Virginia had a somewhat different bone to pick with Ladd. Caplow has in recent years been heading up a massive sociological survey under the title "Middletown III." This governmentally funded program takes a most exacting look at Muncie, Indiana, the original "Middletown" of sociological fame. The findings of Caplow and company on religion in Middletown are analyzed in *All Faithful People* (Minneapolis: University of Minnesota Press, 1983).

Caplow suggested that Ladd may have put too much stress on continuities.

CAPLOW: Ladd tries to establish the point that the level of religion in the United States has remained approximately constant. The fact is I don't think it has remained approximately constant. What data we have does not suggest it has been constant. We have a fair amount of information—that's the point of our Middletown data—that religiosity has very significantly increased since the 1920s. All of us fall into the trap of inventing the past and comparing it with real, empirical data in the present. Organized atheism, for example, was an important force in the 1890s; it is negligible now. Church membership may not be a perfect index, but surely it rose steadily all through the nineteenth century. One concedes too much when one says we're just about as religious as we used to be. We may be a good deal more religious than we used to be.

Ladd did not contest Caplow's reading of changes, but he underscored his interest in making the point that what is called "secularization" does not necessarily come at the expense of religion.

LADD: The gloom about religion's fading role in society, in part represents a misreading of a causal flow. The advent of scientific and industrial and equalitarian revolutions causes secularization. These great revolutionary changes that have defined modernity secularize only in a direct and necessary sense. They make people more expectant and demanding of this world, more able to understand and control aspects of it and insistent that those capacities be enlarged, but not in any inherent sense less receptive to religion.

Paul Johnson did not want the conference to get bogged down in the analysis of numbers. Nor was he sure that it is either helpful or possible to analyze "the authenticity" of the religiousness that survey research reflects. He did urge that we might miss the essential point if we fail to appreciate the dramatic and distinctive ways in which American sensibilities are marked by a "humility and gratitude" that deserve to be called religious.

JOHNSON: Now it may be true that the statistical evidence of continuing faith doesn't really measure the depth of it. And it may be shallower than the statistics suggest in terms of actually influencing the behavior—particularly in making them do things that they really don't want to do just because that is what the churches teach and the Bible teaches and their religion tells them to do, and above all in preventing them from doing things that they do want to do very much. It may be that there is a certain element of weakness there. Nevertheless there is a huge, residual strength of religious feeling in America, a consciousness that America has been a favored country. It may not be the elect nation. It may not even be the "almost-chosen people." But it is a highly favored nation. Americans, although they sometimes appear arrogant to outsiders, are in a deeper sense very grateful for that favor. And they do see it in terms of a God who in handing out the cards has somehow given a very good hand to the Americans. They approach that with a degree of humility and a degree of gratitude. I think that is one of the fundamental elements in the religious spirit in the United States.

Yes, But What Kind of Religion Is It?

George Marsden of Calvin College, one of America's foremost
students of evangelicalism and fundamentalism, is under-
whelmed by much that runs under the banners of religion. "One
person's religion is another person's secularism," he said. "As you
know, the common comment on fundamentalism is that it is just
secularism in disguise. It is a way of endorsing a materialistic,
self-centered lifestyle. And that's something that could be said
about a lot of American Christianity." A good deal of this religion
might be harmful to true religion, he suggested. "Sometimes the
way that secularization advances is by the advance of religion.
That is, from a traditional Christian perspective what happens
is that there is a baptizing of worldly practice. From the perspective of traditional Christianity, the advance of religion might be
a dangerous thing, and that would include civil religion."

Marsden brought up the well-known maxim attributed (some
historians say inaccurately) to President Eisenhower: "Our government makes no sense unless it is founded on a deeply felt
religious faith—and I don't care what it is."

MARSDEN: That "the religion of America is religion" is
what's wrong with American religion. I would be inclined to cite
the Eisenhower quotation as an example of what is wrong on the
basis of, say, the Old Testament prophets criticizing Israel not
for their irreligion but for their religiousness. Their religiousness
is misguided religiousness. You can't imagine an Old Testament
King saying, "Our nation is founded on a deep religious heritage,
and I don't care what it is." By biblical standards that does not
measure up . . . . It might be helpful in survey research on religion to have a category of "folk religion" in talking about American religion—as distinguished from traditional religion. When
you're doing a survey, it's that "folk religion" that tends to come
out—a sincerely but shallowly held religiousness. Maybe that's
what's showing up on the surveys. There might be a lot of religion around, but a decline in traditional religion.

At that a couple of participants protested that we get on to
shaky ground when we presume to be able to measure the depth
or shallowness of the religion of ordinary folk.

Ernest Fortin, a Roman Catholic priest and philosopher at
Boston College, came to Marsden's defense. He suggested that
some judgments, or at least discriminations, can be made and
should be made.

FORTIN: God is on everybody's lips. He has a weekly column in *Time* and *Newsweek*, and you half expect him to make a TV appearance one of these days. But what kind of God is he? It is all right to find out how often people pray to God, but to which kind of god are they praying? He seems to be a very benevolent God who is willing to tolerate an awful lot of things. Religion does seem to be trimming its sails a great deal. With the kind of religion that has made its peace with the modern world, I don't see that there is any great conflict necessarily between modernization and religion. What we have seen, in fact, is the gradual erosion of the family, and that has reached enormous proportions. Superstition is on the rise as much as religion. And I would hesitate to say that our moral standards have improved a great deal in the past few years. You don't have to be familiar with Times Square or the "Combat Zone" in Boston to observe that.

Stanley Rothman, a social scientist at the University of Massachusetts who has done pioneering work on Jews in American society, took a similar view.

ROTHMAN: In a public-opinion survey people are asked, "Do you believe in hard work?" Sure, everyone may mouth that. But there is a difference between saying that and actually doing it, having the capacity and willingness to postpone gratification until certain points and maintaining a kind of meticulousness about one's work. And I would say the same thing about religious attitudes among the population as a whole. Modernization of the West has led to the erosion of the traditional structures and beliefs which were associated with the West in an earlier period—namely, Christianity and Judaism. There is a general indication that the kinds of attitudes, orientations, and restraints associated with traditional religiosity in this society have broken down and are continuing to erode. I am thinking about things like divorce. In traditional Christian and Jewish attitudes, you did not get divorced. You simply didn't. Now there is evidence that people no longer take religion so seriously, unless they redefine it in some ways. I think there has been a general redefinition, not among the whole population, but among substantial segments of the population, so as to fit religion into their own wishes and desires. Religion does not play this role in guiding everybody. Unfortunately this cannot be proved with data.

Rothman did not want to say that popular religion is not sincerely held, or authentic, or whatever, but he did wonder whether it is always recognizable as the religion that it claims to be.

ROTHMAN: At least what's happening is a decline in support for traditional structures and religious attitudes. In America this has taken a different form than in Europe partly because of the accommodative quality of our culture. At Smith College during the 1960s I overheard one young radical say to another, "This place is terrible. You really can't find any way to mount a demonstration, because they're always giving in." This is one of the characteristics of American society. There are strong signs that at least the traditional religious values are undergoing modification and change. Earlier in American history the pursuit of happiness assumed that you don't get divorced, you don't covet your neighbor's wife. These were underlying assumptions. Now what has happened generally is that the pursuit of happiness means any pursuit of happiness, and God had better adapt to what we think is the appropriate pursuit of happiness. There comes a point, however, that this new religion is not the religion of your fathers. This is not "the old-time religion."

The conversation turned to whether it is a fatal flaw in the vaunted religious revival that religion is so much attached to material well-being. Paul Johnson did not speak in praise of materialism, but neither was he sure that materialism is the problem.

JOHNSON: When people point to the contrast between the American religious spirit and materialism, I'm not at all sure that is the right contrast. In a sense materialism can easily be channeled into religious practice. People make their pile, and then they want to devote it to charitable causes, to religious purposes, just as Norman knights in the tenth and eleventh and early twelfth centuries would battle their way to riches and then found an abbey. The real danger in America is the contrast between religion and hedonism—this strong feeling among Americans that the pursuit of happiness is a natural right. That is in conflict with the religious spirit. And that is part of the problem now, today. It explains the superficiality which is characteristic of American religious belief; people want to go to church to believe in the afterlife, and they don't want to sacrifice their right to happiness. That is incompatible with the Christian spirit. We live in a veil of tears; we don't have a right to happiness. Happiness is a felicity which may come along as a result of divine providence, but it's not something we have a right to.

Happiness has come to be defined negatively as a kind of right not to suffer, or even to be inconvenienced, said Midge Decter. And, while ideas are critically important, she suggested this also has something to do with the material circumstances to which we have become accustomed and are inclined to claim as ours by right.

DECTER: I mean attitudes to things like pain and suffering. You can't expect to have doubled the median income in a society in a quarter of a century without having some powerful impact. The question is: What is the nature of that impact? As a society at this point, we are conducting a public discussion, a public, political discussion, on whether the life of this or that newborn baby is a life worth living. This is a discussion that's being presented to the courts and the medical authorities, and it's being debated on op-ed pages. The fact that this is considered a kind of open, debatable question, which judges should contribute to and doctors should contribute to and social philosophers should contribute to, the fact that we are even having this discussion is not only the result of what technology has done for us but also its spiritual impact on us. It is an unwritten premise in this society that suffering or pain or death is a kind of active injustice against us. Diseases are supposed to be done away with. Everyone who dies is considered to be maltreated by society. Something should have been done to prevent this. If death is an injustice, certainly pain, discomfort, misery are—why should we have them?

Talk about the "Me Generation" has been rampant for years, and Mark Noll of Wheaton College observed that this perverse individualism may be at the heart of what troubles thoughtful people about current religiosities. Noll noted that the Reformation is frequently blamed for the rise of individualism in religion but that the classical reformers, at least, assumed that religion has a public character that transcends the individual. This is equally true in the American Protestant tradition with figures such as Cotton, Winthrop, Edwards, and the American Samuel Johnson. Might not the new thing be this relentless turning in upon the individual? "Might not such an individualized religion be, in effect, the functional equivalent of European secularization?" Noll asked. Richard Neuhaus agreed that, at least in our public life, it seems possible to operate with a "practical atheism" despite the fact that most of the individuals who constitute "the public" profess an intense religiosity.

Steven Tipton of Emory University is a member of the team that produced the much-discussed study *Habits of the Heart*, and he believes that study has an important bearing on our subject. He emphasized that we must take seriously institutional arrangements and the ways in which "social placement" influences our thinking about religion and morality.

TIPTON: America is both persistently religious and intensely secular. How? There is an institutional contraction of religion in the process of institutional differentiation that does make a society modern and that goes along with a kind of cultural pluralism. Call it the division of labor and the multiplication of morality. That does not necessarily mean that there is less religion around in the hearts and minds of individuals. So ninety-five percent of us can still believe in God. The problem is the multiplication of morality that goes along with the division of labor. Here the question is: What is the proper institutional location and salience of religious ideas, especially religious ethics, or the religious sources of moral understanding—particularly moral understanding about how ought we to live together? And then more specifically, what is the place of those religious ideas and ethics in the polity itself, and what is their relationship to nonreligious moral ideas and understandings?

The approach advanced by Tipton makes distinctions between individualisms. For example, there is utilitarian individualism (looking out for Number One) and expressive individualism (I wanna be Me). More constructively, there is also republican individualism, which stresses participation in a polity of moral significance, and biblical individualism, which lifts up the note of ultimate accountability. So it is not very helpful, says Tipton, to say that the problem is that religion is too individualistic. We have to ask what kind of individualism is being reinforced.

TIPTON: The religious views that people hold may not supply direct answers to this or that public question, but they do help shape the way that individuals position themselves toward others. Religious opinions and attitudes, no matter how cleverly aggregated and disaggregated, are only a sort of backdrop to the real discussion about what religion has got to do with the way we argue over and live out our ideas of right and wrong, good and bad, what makes life worth living, and what makes a society worth living in and working for.

Religion as "a sort of backdrop" may seem somewhat pallid. But Tipton wanted to stress that people do not, in everyday fact, move from religious premise to moral conclusion. He cited studies demonstrating that in the abortion debate, for example, activists on both sides are shaped by their "social situation," at least in large part. Pro-choice activists tend to be upper-middle-class, well-educated, professional career women married to professionals, making more than $50,000 a year, and religiously uncommitted. The contrast on each of these scores with pro-life activists is dramatic.

TIPTON: It is not just a question of interests and the way that different people from different social locations or positions differently define interests. It's the way that a way of life establishes a social context in which an idea of abortion and marriage rings true or not so true. And in this case ideals of marriage for pro-choice types are seen mainly in terms of a relationship between two autonomous individuals that's predicated on romantic intimacy. So it's expressive individualism, not just utilitarian. And then also it's a kind of contractual relationship with high regard for procedural justice and negotiation and equal rights. For the counterparts there is a much more "traditional" notion of marriage that's not predicated mainly on romantic intimacy and rights to occupational as well as emotional self-fulfillment, but much more predicated on procreation and parenthood. Motherhood is central to this idea of marriage, and it involves a differentiation in terms of duties and authority between the sexes. So we get a picture of the way that moral ideas and social experience are tied together, and the complexity of that kind of interlinking.

Everett Ladd readily acknowledged the complexity, but he was not easily discouraged. He suggested that it might be the case that the vitality of American religion is demonstrated by its flexibility in adjusting to diverse situations. "Is there any reason why religion cannot adapt successfully, providing that the people running it are smart enough and work hard enough, to a highly individualist society?" he asked. "Of course religion can adapt that way, and does," Noll responded, "but is it *good* religion?" Rothman made the point in a different way, arguing that those who ask whether religion can adapt thereby indicate that they are assuming "that religion is a mythology, a myth, like any other myth." Myths, it is understood, are different from truths. Myths are useful or not depending on whether they serve our purposes: myths serve us, whereas we must serve truths.

Ed Hindson of Liberty University in Lynchburg, Virginia, noted that some communities understand that distinction better than others.

HINDSON: The resistance to that adaptation to cultural fashions is stronger in the fundamentalist-evangelical-charismatic community than it is in the mainline community. Where in mainline Protestantism do you have the kind of thing going on to prevent divorce, for instance, that you have in evangelical circles—the Bill Gothard–James Dobson types of things where you have twenty thousand people gathered in an auditorium listening to somebody articulate biblical principles of family living in an attempt to halt divorce? One of the reasons there is a strong appeal within conservative religion is that people are finding in a sense more help in dealing with that kind of thing.

Ed Dobson, Hindson's colleague and also vice president of the Moral Majority, acknowledged that fundamentalism's service to the truth is not always so unequivocal.

DOBSON: Fundamentalists have been perceived by people outside of our faith community, whether correctly or incorrectly, as having all of the answers to all of life's problems. I see within fundamentalism, especially in the last four or five years, apparently contradictory trends in regards to the culture, modernization, modernity, and secularism. On the one hand, I see us in clear confrontation with the culture. The clearest illustration of that is the whole abortion issue, where we find ourselves at odds with what are perceived as secularist values in regards to human life. In that dimension we've made a clear impact on the political process and we don't intend to go away. Underneath all of that, I find that we are, within our community, also struggling with adaptation to the culture. That is especially clear on the whole issue of divorce. Ten years ago in fundamentalist churches divorce was unheard of, and our edicts against divorce were simple: God is against it, we're against it, don't do it. That was sufficient. All of that has changed. The culture is impacting on us. The general forty percent divorce rate is no longer a problem that "they," the nonfundamentalists, have. It is now a problem that we have.

This train of conversation had been kicked off by George Marsden's reflections on the "shallowness" of American religion, and Midge Decter returned the group to that. It is not simply American religion that is shallow, Decter said.

DECTER: Marsden alluded to the shallowness, the lack of depth of American religion, but the same can be said of American culture in comparison with European culture. A better term than *shallowness* might be *callowness*. American novels seem thin when compared with works in the great British and Russian traditions of fiction. There is a kind of innocence in American culture about the darker side of life and man. This may be a unique expression and condition of the way American society has put itself together as a social reality.

This prompted some objections and the invocation of Herman Melville's name. Was Decter really saying that *Moby Dick* is shallow? Not shallow, she said, but callow, yes. And, she wanted to know, what exceptions are there other than Melville? The objections to her indictment were not pressed.

If *callow* means "immature" and "green" and "lacking in depth," Brian Benestad of Scranton University was prepared to agree with Decter, although he was not sure whether it's the religion that does it to the culture or the other way around.

BENESTAD: Tocqueville said that in no country in the civilized world is less attention paid to philosophy than in the United States. It is an interesting statement to read to students and ask them if they think that's a compliment or an insult. They're not quite sure. It may have something to do with the thinness of our religion. We have a problem injecting mind into our religion. It tends to get modified by current affairs. Today our religion gets transmogrified into politics or psychology, or something else.

Exactly, said Marsden. Religion is presented as being useful, rather than demanding any depth commitment. And that is relevant to interpreting the indices of "religious growth," such as church membership.

MARSDEN: As Professor Caplow observes, religion does seem to be expanding by a lot of the measures that we find when looking at American Life. The most puzzling of them is church membership statistics. And by that statistic religion seems to have increased to be much greater in American life in the twentieth century than in the nineteenth or the eighteenth centuries. But the obvious point is that it's an awful lot easier to become a member of a church today than it was in the 1920s, and it was a lot easier in the 1920s than it was in the 1820s, and it was a lot easier in the 1820s than it was in the 1720s. In the 1620s it was almost impossible to become a church member. For the Puritans the whole of sanctification was expected as a prerequisite to church membership; you had to have reached a level of sanctification that only a few saints ever got to. Only gradually that declined to the opposite—what we have today, where rather than ask people to give up anything to become Christians, they're promised everything. Of course this religion is going to grow.

People do not always understand their religious needs, Michael Novak of the American Enterprise Institute observed. If the individual has a hard time in discerning spiritual truth, it is little wonder that we have a doubly hard time trying to discern what is really happening with people in that part of their life they call religious.

NOVAK: There used to be a language in talking about religion which has pretty much dropped out of sight. It was the language of the cure of souls, the discernment of spirits, the spiritual direction. The assumption was that the way people speak about themselves and even think about themselves may be wrong, may be misleading. They may be self-deceived. It is the task of a person very skilled in religious experience to help people see through this and not be misled by the views which people have of themselves. This is important since much of the discussion has had to do with measuring religion and its ups and downs. It brings to light that the very thing we're trying to deal with— religion—has so many different dimensions to it, it's very hard to get hold of it and be clear. Religion is such a complicated phenomenon that it's not always clear if it's in advance or in decline. To reach the discernment of spirit that would allow us to say which is which is very, very difficult. And it's a process which is extended over time.

In the course of the conversation, possibly apropos of nothing in particular, Neuhaus shared what he had been told was the archetypically Jewish telegram: START WORRYING. LETTER TO FOLLOW. Toward the end of this session dealing with the survey research data on religion in America, Midge Decter picked up on that.

DECTER: Being Jewish, I am afraid that I am required to say, "Start worrying. Letter to follow." Clearly, something is wrong. I don't think we'd be here today if we did not all feel something is wrong. I do not presume to know what that something is. We use terms like *secular humanism* and *secularization*, but one never sees the word *atheism* used. That's a very, very important term. It has gone out of style. Somehow I find that it relates somewhere to what seems to be wrong. That is, I think what is called "secularization" has a more profound effect on people's attitudes than Ladd's data, by themselves, can possibly indicate. A man can pray at least once a day or say he believes in the life to come and go to church and nevertheless have certain attitudes to life that are profoundly antireligious. The question is: What are the strains of attitude in American culture that are leaving us all with the feeling that something is wrong? Now it may just be that people are inclined to think that their own period is always worse than others—the nostalgia factor. If that were the only problem, we wouldn't all be sitting here and we wouldn't all have been troubled over the past few decades about something going wrong. We do perceive some spiritual difficulty that we are having in this society having to do with deep attitudes to life—not to one's minister or to one's church or even to God but to the nature of human existence. That dimension is missing from the Ladd data.

American People, American Elite

Stanley Rothman's work on the "new class" is a standard point of reference in any discussion of how elite groups shape American culture. What is called the new class is composed of people in the knowledge industry—in universities, communications media, and much of government employment—who are alienated from, and frequently hostile to, the values of the business class. They constitute an elite that is often contrasted with "the real America."

ROTHMAN: The new class is made up of strategic elites. They are not even new elites. Some of them are old elites which have changed. They are very secular, many of them, and also quite liberal and cosmopolitan. Aside from military and businessmen and to a lesser extent bureaucrats, they tend to be a fairly secular group. Hollywood people, television people, even corporate lawyers, journalists, public-interest-group leaders, they are all quite secular by various measures.

Everett Ladd did not disagree, but he cautioned against elite-bashing, citing current studies that highlight "the steady march for the last quarter century of elites that are militantly secular." Ladd said he shares this rather gloomy estimate of the intellectual elite and has a much more favorable view of the wisdom of the general public. On the other hand, he is not so sure that the march is all that steady.

LADD: Why has this aggressive, near consensual, intellectually held ideology, which has crowded religion out of academe and high culture, found so few converts among those exposed to college training? Among the people thirty-four and under who are college graduates, the proportion who say they pray regularly, at least daily, is slightly higher than among their noncollege counterparts. The same thing holds for the proportion who regularly attend religious services: slightly higher among the college cohorts than among the noncollege.

Neuhaus remarked, half jokingly, that maybe the good news is that the colleges are obviously not teaching very effectively.

Since Diane Ravitch works at Columbia Teachers College, it is not surprising that she had an opinion on this.

RAVITCH: While it may be true that the college-educated populace is much like the rest on many of these measures on religion, politics, and so on, nonetheless there is within the college-educated population a distinct elite of disproportionate influence and power in our society. When I was out doing a series of lectures in 1984 before the election, I was struck by the differences between elite campuses and regular campuses. The Ivy League campuses in the straw polls voted overwhelmingly for Mondale—like seventy-five percent for Mondale. Yet on every campus I visited in the South and Midwest, the figures were exactly reversed; no one there was for Mondale other than the faculty, and the faculties were in despair because they had not done a better job of liberating their students. Even in colleges like Furman University, the same faculty attitudes were present that I had found at Yale and Harvard, but not among the students.

But there is college education and then there is college education, Peter Berger observed: "What are the data in terms of different fields of academic discipline? Because 'college educated' does not tell us anything. You can have a college degree in engineering. Are there data which discriminate, say within the same university, between students in the engineering school and students in political science?" Ladd had an answer to that: "Yes, sociology undergraduates overall look different than engineering undergraduates. But I have not found any way in working with data on young, college-educated people to break out any large group that looks like foot soldiers of the approach that new-class theory has described." To this Rothman added, "It is commonplace that students who were liberal already go into the social sciences. There is self-selection. The academic situation as a whole does not look that much to the left or toward the liberal. But the social scientists do. I have a comparison between students in business school and students in the Columbia School of Journalism. They look very, very different, obviously."

In the course of earlier conversation George Marsden had remarked that his Christian commitment meant that he does not approach some questions with strict objectivity. George Gallup, head of America's premier polling organization, suggested that the perspective of some disciplines is badly skewed at precisely this point.

GALLUP: Dr. Marsden apologized for being "nonobjective." It should be just as natural to apologize if you're nonreligious. In the situation of sociology today we see what we might be seeing in journalism. People are generally coming from a nonreligious perspective, which is no more respectable a sociological position than to be religious. The tendency, when you come from the nonreligious perspective, is to dissect this weird phenomenon of religion in Americans' lives. If you come from at least a potentially theistic position, you then have the advantage of asking key, new, good, fresh questions about people's spiritual lives. You have a fresh approach denied you if you don't. You have sympathy for all points of view, which you don't otherwise. We should urge that we encourage sociologists and other observers who come from the religious traditions to give that freshness to our approach to this study.

The University of California at Davis may be one place where something new is stirring, according to sociologist Jay Mechling.

MECHLING: It may be that the influence on religion of the secular humanist or positivist or whatever is being exaggerated right now, because things might be changing. I only have my experience at Davis, which is a highly scientific, engineering campus, to go on. There are either evangelical or fundamentalist members of the science and math and engineering departments who witness during committee meetings. And this is creating quite a stir.

And it is not only the faculty, he noted: "In reading lots of student applications to Davis from people who are coming into the sciences, I note lots of people writing in their scholarship essays that they have a personal relationship to God and see their vocation as somehow serving God and so on. These are not people going into history or English; these are people who are going to become engineers."

Within religious communities themselves something strange seems to be happening in connection with the elite, Theodore Caplow observed.

CAPLOW: A recent book on European values makes the comment that all the European survey data show the persistence of a tight relationship between religious affiliation and political position, with a reasonably small margin of error. If you know the religious behavior of a European, you can accurately predict his politics, often his specific party affiliation and voting behavior, and vice versa. This is not at all true in the United States. It is not even remotely true. The correlation is negligible and unstable.

The studies done in the 1950s showed that by and large the clergy did have more of a tendency to fall onto a particular point on the political spectrum than the laity did. It wasn't a very strong connection, but to some extent you could locate the clergy of each denomination on the political spectrum much better than you could the laity. And by and large they tended to be more conservative. The laity always went to the center, but the clergy were conservative in the sense that they had a narrower range of variation. Something has happened to that relationship that is almost inexplicable. In every American denomination in which this has been tried, the clergy now stand to the left on the political spectrum.

George Gallup did an amazing study with respect to the revised prayerbook, the Book of Common Prayer, of the Episcopal Church. It showed about eighty percent of the clergy in favor of the revision and about eighty percent of the laity opposed. The same general pattern runs from Baptists to Lutherans, from sectarian groups to Moslems. The clergy in general stand to the left and have something of a distinct political orientation. Whereas, for all practical purposes, the rank and file, the lay members of the denominations, cannot be located on the political spectrum by reference to their religious behavior.

Ernest Fortin suggested that maybe the secularizing elite of the universities are more effective in reaching the clergy.

FORTIN: Somehow church leaders became vulnerable. In our time they have succumbed to the power of public opinion to a large extent. By public opinion I don't simply mean what the large number of people in our land happen to think about this or that matter. The public opinion in question emanates from university circles. In many cases that is where the thinking is done. Religious leaders tend to be more teachable than the people. So you end up with eighty percent of the clergy being liberal and eighty percent of the faithful being conservative. All sorts of new tensions begin to develop.

The black churches are not immune to the pattern under discussion, according to Robert Woodson, who heads the National Center for Neighborhood Enterprise and is in the forefront of efforts to chart a postliberal course for black advancement.

WOODSON: Many of the mainline black churches that participate in the National Council of Churches have more in common with their ecumenical partners than they do with their own people—I mean, the grass roots, poor people. Ministers are now to the left of their congregations. I have great concern about the move of the fundamentalists toward greater intellectual acceptance. With that comes professionalization. As a consequence of that, they do become disconnected from their historical moorings and disconnected, therefore, from the people. The same thing is true in the civil rights community. You look at the polls and the positions that they take are far to the left of the population—on busing, on abortion, on school prayer. Even with the Hispanic community—if you'd poll the Hispanic community and ask it if it thinks the United States should set up some different policies to regulate the flow of immigrants from Mexico, it would say Yes and the leadership would say No. It is a question of whose will prevails in this environment. Apparently the professionals dominate the decision-making process, because they are the experts, they are the people Congress listens to, they are the people who seem to drive policy.

All of this, said Woodson, has very practical, and for the most part depressing, implications.

WOODSON: This move toward greater cooperation and intellectualization and professionalization—when it impacts upon my area, it has a devastating effect on social policy. There was a time, for example, when abandoned children were cared for primarily by the church. The church provided the money for services and determined the rules. And therefore it was not in the church's economic interest to maintain children away from stable homes. It wasn't practical to do that; it was more expensive. But eventually the church organizations moved into the state economy. Jewish, Catholic, and Protestant organizations eventually moved into the state economy, and became somewhat detached from their religious base until they've reached the point today that most of them operate like any other public or private agency, conforming to the same rules. Ninety to one hundred percent of the moneys for these so-called religious agencies comes not from the church but from the state.

When I first went to Washington, D.C., eight years ago, every weekend for six consecutive weekends a black teenager hanged himself in the care of the child-welfare-juvenile-justice system. The response of the public was that we've got to have better training for professionals, smaller case loads, and so on. If the Klan had come to Washington and assaulted one youngster, there would have been massive civil rights demonstrations, the council of churches would have put up some money, folks would have come to town on buses, and we would have had a big demonstration. But six kids can die in the present system, and little happens. According to our studies one-third of our abandoned children end up graduating into the jails, so we're incubating tomorrow's criminals at public expense in the name of saving children, and the mortality rate is twice that of the national average. All of these things we're doing are destroying families in the name of helping them. Some of your churches are killing us.

How Exceptional Is America, and Why?

From the impact of elite worldviews upon poor Americans the discussion returned to the perhaps larger question of why, with respect to religion, America is so different from other countries—and whether it is in fact still all that different.

PETER BERGER: There has been the proposition, which in an earlier part of my own life I supported, that modernization causes secularization. I think that we can say that the data that Ladd cites and that Caplow has been producing falsifies that proposition. Period. It has to be thrown out. I have thrown it out. It's wrong. Because if that were a generally tenable theory, the

United States is an important enough case where you have to decide it has been falsified. Fine. That's how scientific understanding proceeds. But on the other hand we have these comparative data. And let's limit ourselves to advanced, industrialized societies. If you take North American and West European societies—except for Ireland—the United States is absolutely by itself in religiosity. The logic here is that while the proposition has been falsified, enough countries in this group of countries seem to have this high correlation between modernization and secularization that what one really has to explain is the exceptionalism of the American case. Why are Americans so different from Swedes?

In this session of the conference the focus was on the paper by Paul Johnson. Johnson was insistent that we not lose sight of the historical formation of American self-understandings.

JOHNSON: Lincoln used the phrase "the almost-chosen people." What he probably meant by that was akin to the doctrine of original sin. We're made in God's image, but there's a flaw. It's as though one is looking into a hideously distorted mirror. The image of God is there, but it's distorted in the human face. And we call that *original sin*, that terrible flaw. I think perhaps what Lincoln meant was that Americans were a specially favored people; God had looked kindly on them, but there was a radical flaw in their national personality. The flaw may be materialism, or what have you. And that took away from the nation its special, elect mission.

Those things that seem to characterize the American reality are historically dependent on one another to a degree that is not sufficiently appreciated, Johnson suggested.

JOHNSON: Looking at the tripod of democracy, capitalism, and Christianity, one can say that both democracy and capitalism have their roots in Christianity. Democracy is something inherent in Judeo-Christianity in this sense. The Jewish religion, as developed in pre-Mosaic and Mosaic times, was a communal religion, based upon the notion of equality. Most religions up till then and many religions since then have assumed that the temporal ruler was in some sense a god. This was the essence of the ancient Egyptian religion and most of the Middle Eastern religions. The Jews for the first time drew an absolute distinction between God and man. And that really is the core of Judaism to this day. God is quite different. Man is in no way part of God. There's no question of an apotheosis. And because man and God are quite different, men are therefore equal. And there was this very, very strong communal sense, community sense, in Judaism which Christianity inherited, because Christianity grew up out of the Jewish Diaspora. Therefore, this sense of the separation between God and man remained a salient characteristic despite the doctrine of the Incarnation, almost because of the doctrine of the Incarnation.

In all Christian societies there is the root belief in the equality before God of all men. Once you have equality before God in a religious sense, ultimately you get it in a secular and a political sense too. Capitalism also has its roots in Christianity. We were brought up to believe, when we were in school, in Max Weber's thesis of the Protestant ethic, the salvation ethic, and all that, but of course Christianity's relations with progressive business practice go back much deeper than that. I believe they go back almost to the roots of Christianity, because Christianity inherited from the Jews a sense that to do business was to do God's will, if you did it according to God's law. Great philosophers like Maimonides engaged in business activities throughout their lives. In medieval Christianity, after all, if you take the Cistercians, a late eleventh-century, early twelfth-century order, they were the first great international corporation. They developed all over Europe. One estate produced capital funds to finance the other and so on. They were the first multinational corporation.

Throughout the Middle Ages this association between business and Christianity persisted and developed. The late thirteenth-century, fourteenth-century, and fifteenth-century guilds, business guilds, were very highly Christianized. They had their own chapels and endowments and so on. But they were very much business communities. This long predates any kind of Calvinistic addition. The roots of capitalism lie in Christianity. And the roots of democracy lie in Christianity.

Neuhaus referred to the scripture appointed that day for morning prayer in the community of which he is part.

NEUHAUS: In Ephesians 6 you have this marvelous passage where Paul is laying out the hierarchical sense of duty that wives should obey husbands and so on. And then he says, "as for you, slaves, you should obey your masters," and "you, masters, should not threaten your slaves!" (I think the proper word there would be *humiliate*, or "threaten them in a humiliating way.") "For you must remember that your God and theirs will hold you both to judgment." It's an extraordinary statement of the roots of some kind of democratic idea that everything was relativized by this notion of a transcendent judgment.

For better or for worse, says Theodore Caplow, this sense of transcendent judgment has made Americans a moralistic, if not moral, people.

CAPLOW: The whole picture of the American experience in these papers is that we do our politics differently than other nations. There is really no resemblance between the basic style of political controversy over social issues in the United States and that which happens in Western Europe or elsewhere in the world. They are concerned with justice, equality, fraternity, but not often with morality. Whereas the history of this country is simply one issue after another presented in terms of the cases that the common morality didn't cover. The issues are always moral, and they often lead to bloodshed. The first half of the nineteenth century was, of course, obsessed with just such an issue; the common morality covered everything but slavery. And there in perfect righteousness, the two sides confronted each other appealing to the same religious tradition. The second half of the nineteenth century had a whole welter of issues—on the rights of labor and women and prohibition and temperance—where again two sets of rights confronted each other in terms which, even if they draw from anti-religious thinkers, were essentially always appeals to the common morality with religious grounds. We have it today on abortion, capital punishment, and all the presently really divisive issues. That kind of argumentation, moralities in conflict, is as American as apple pie and as old as the Republic. Both sides are convinced of the consistency of their positions with the mainstream of Christian doctrine.

Against the view of many Europeans, Johnson contended that this moral posture of Americans toward the world has not led to the vices associated with "imperialism." America has undoubtedly done some very stupid and even wrong things, but the American intention is generally one of generosity. "Of course it is true that when countries get the feeling that they have a divine mission, they're liable to invade other people's territory to spread the word. But I honestly don't think that has ever been the pattern in America. Even the President McKinley case with the Philippines was an expression rather of generosity than imperialism."

Robert Wuthnow of Princeton was uneasy about Johnson's

way of telling the story. He made several comments, in part by way of protest, but also to lift up some apparent ambiguities, even contradictions, in American self-understanding and behavior.

WUTHNOW: The religious myth of American origins as pictured in Johnson's paper is a story that many people don't feel comfortable with. It somehow doesn't ring true to many people. The Vietnam experience, which may have affected people of my cohort—I happened to be in college and graduate school at the time—more than others, and the gap between rhetoric and reality in American policy deeply affected many. Perhaps European observers have not fully appreciated yet the effect of the Vietnam experience on our understanding. Let me give some examples of ways in which the story differs.

In a very interesting recent book entitled *The American Style of Foreign Policy*, Robert Dallek sees McKinley as a very religiously motivated person but also suggests that McKinley was the last such president, at least as far as American foreign policy is concerned. There has been a steady secularization of American policy, oriented much more around material and pragmatic legitimations—instead of religious ones. The issue of immigration as something that symbolizes America's religious freedom is also somewhat tarnished nowadays as we look at some of the polls that Everett Ladd has run in *Public Opinion* recently. They show that Americans are, maybe always were, but especially now that we have polls to show it, rather mean-minded and nasty toward immigrants and not terribly anxious to welcome them. At the same time, as far as the immigrants are concerned, I'm not sure whether the attraction of America is religious liberty, if that really is what brings people across the Rio Grande and from Cuba.

Another example is the article Stanley Hoffman did in the *New York Review of Books* around the time of the 1984 Republican Convention. In it he suggested that for a long time there had been two myths that had formulated Americans' conceptions of themselves in the world—one, the myth of ourselves as missionaries who do in fact uphold the example of religion to the rest of the world; the other, the image of the *High Noon* sheriff who's ready to go shoot it out with the bad guys. His suggestion was that neither of those myths animates us as a people anymore. Instead he pointed to the Los Angeles Olympics as an example where we symbolically sit back and receive a mild euphoria because some of our athletes are doing well in the world. About all we can muster, he suggests, is a mild euphoria.

Think about religion relative to some of the other legitimating myths that we use as a country. For example, there are recent survey questions that ask the American people, "What do you think is the biggest determining factor of America's role in the world in the next decade or so?" Religion ranks way down. Technology and science rank way up. There are other Gallup questions that ask people to say how important certain things are to their own sense of well-being or their own values. Again, in that kind of ranking religion ranks way down. I think in one list there were twelve such values: something like "following God's will" ranked seventh out of twelve, whereas things like freedom, hard work, and success were up at the top. Other polls that have been done in Europe asked Europeans what they think of America. It isn't that America's unique because it's religious; it's more that America has freedom.

Clifford Geertz and other anthropologists often argue that what happens during a period of cultural change is not so much that the old myths get displaced but that new myths grow up on top of them, and more or less devalue them. Part of our crisis of exceptionalism may be that we are coming to be a more materialistic or more technologically mythologized people or simply a more pragmatic people at the same time that we are a very religious people.

Os Guiness is an English evangelical author who is currently in America writing a book about the oddities of religion and culture in this society. He is not at all sure that what used to be meant by American exceptionalism still holds.

GUINESS: The earliest Puritan case for American exceptionalism very few Americans now support, in the strong form of equating America with Old Testament Israel. That theologically strong form has collapsed. Plus you have a secular veto today about any mention of that sort of thing in public. Then you have various other strands in American history: some of the exceptionalisms were based on geography, some on economics, some on history. All those other more pragmatic grounds have declined. So I've heard Europeans suggest recently that there are only two areas today where America is strikingly exceptional: in the levels of its immigration, but supremely in religion. And yet even the grounds for the religious distinction, for many people, have collapsed. And it's very significant that since Vietnam the political liberals have been conspicuously silent in articulating American policy in its old ways. So you have a large segment of the American population that no longer believes those things.

There's surely a much greater crisis of exceptionalism than we've looked at. The loss of the sense of exceptionalism must mean something to Americans—even secular Americans—certainly in the way they articulate their policy in the world.

The last several hours had heard some hard words about the elite. Mark Noll of Wheaton was not eager to praise the elite, but he thought it important to underscore the importance of leadership that transcends the vulgar democracy that appeals only to the views of "the people."

NOLL: What makes democracy work in the United States, what makes even voluntaristic religion work, is something that transcends the voice of the people. In the American Revolution it's an elite group moving people to what's good for them, and it probably was good for them. In the Civil War it's Lincoln seeing that both sides are praying to the same God and yet the will of God is above and beyond; it transcends the will of both. I wonder if the juncture between democracy and the religiosity that has prevailed in America is not a far more complex and a far more mysterious thing than what we sometimes think it might be.

America, Democracy, and Divine Intent

Noll's caution on the dangers of a vulgarized democratic notion that "the people" are always right led into a discussion of different notions of democracy. Elaborating on the argument he had presented in his paper—that America is a nation on purpose and by purpose—Neuhaus said, "We are not simply born into America; we buy into it." And buying into it, he noted, involves buying into some critical ideas about democratic governance. He maintained that in this century there have been very few Christian thinkers who have attempted a theologically serious explanation of the democratic idea. Jacques Maritain, Reinhold Niebuhr, and John Courtney Murray all addressed the question, but for whatever reason none did it with the systematic thoroughness that the question requires. Neuhaus acknowledged that anything like a "theology of democracy" makes some people very nervous.

NEUHAUS: Part of that is the fear that a theology of or a theological legitimation for the democratic idea and its American embodiment partakes of the temptation of idolatry and immediately conjures images of "Manifest Destiny" and the like. But it is precisely in the absence of a transcendent point of reference that the danger of idolatry arises. Because then, if you are going to articulate anything and bring it to consciousness so to speak, you have to articulate a self-validating reason for the American experiment which I don't think can be done except idolatrously. Or else you simply have to supress the question of purpose, and that leads to the kind of fragmentation and moral evacuation of the political enterprise itself. Politics becomes simply a matter of brokering interests. We have to be able again to propose in public something about the purpose that partakes of something like a compelling and even ultimate purpose. But I readily admit it's a very risky enterprise.

Steven Tipton had earlier raised the issue of how "morality" enters into the abortion debate in different ways from the different sides of that debate. The problem of the moral legitimation of democracy, several participants noted, is not simply a problem of the absence of moral language or reasoning. We are awash in moral and moralistic language, Peter Berger noted. Neuhaus agreed but observed that in the abortion debate, for example, we have quite different kinds of moral language engaged. "The pro-choice position," he said, "almost always employs the moral language of rights, whereas the pro-life position employs a morality of duty." The morality of duty has a number of strengths, he went on to suggest: it can encompass the acceptance of suffering, and it can also encompass a sense of obligation to a certain vision of how society ought to be ordered—for instance, an obligation to the democratic experiment.

Much of the discussion now turned to an exchange between Marsden and Neuhaus, reflecting differences implicit in their papers.

MARSDEN: It might be that the naked public square is better thought of as a symbol of what's right in the American tradition than what's wrong. That there can be a sympathy toward religion but then a careful distancing of religion from public philosophy is good. Despite the moral relativism, there are things that people agree on. There might be some basis for a public philosophy appealing to some kind of natural, moral sensibilities that people have. Even on the abortion issue, it's not that we lack a language for the public discourse. Everyone agrees that it's wrong to kill innocent persons. The disagreement is on the more technical point of who's a person.

Neuhaus responded that he was not at all sure that "everyone agrees" that it is wrong to kill innocent human beings; he suggested that recourse to the vague language of "personhood" is frequently an evasion of that reality. Marsden was nonetheless anxious about what an alternative to the naked public square might mean.

MARSDEN: If you get the combination of political power and God's authority, then you have a very dangerous kind of situation. Because you have absolute political authority and power and you know that you are right. The next step is a kind of totalitarianism, because why would you tolerate people who are wrong on this or that issue when you know on God's authority that you are right? Once you have God on your side, there's no room for compromise. The genius of the democratic-pluralistic polity is some willingness to compromise.

Neuhaus responded that compromise is indeed essential in democratic politics, as is reverence for those with whom one disagrees, precisely because it is God's will that all social orders should remain open to an understanding of his ultimate truth, which none of us now securely or completely possesses. In addition, the individual, no matter how wrongheaded he or she may be, remains nonetheless a bearer of the divine image and has the infinite potential of conversion to the One who is the Truth.

Tipton was sympathetic to Marsden's concern about absolutisms in the public square, but he noted that "there can be a kind of absolutistic orthodoxy of bureaucratic individualism or secular scientific ideology just as there can be an absolutism of one or another kind of religious belief."

TIPTON: What George Marsden most fears is basically aggressive sects. You see that one solution is the Hobbesian solution. Hobbes was no fool. He says precisely because society can't reach a moral consensus, we can't really agree about the true scriptures and the moral truth implied or commanded thereby, and therefore we need not only a social contract but also a state church. The political sovereign is also the "sovereign prophet" of a state church. That's one way to go. The other way to go, when you're faced with this kind of predicament in classical social theory, is Adam Smith. Here the oppressive and conflicting authority of princes who present themselves as God's chosen prophets are cast aside in favor of few laws, free markets, and interpersonal exchange. So we all become one through thousands upon thousands of face-to-face, sympathetic exchanges, not just economic exchanges. That's what Marsden is afraid of—aggressive sects. To deal with that without winding up with a state church, secular or quasi-Christian, he's willing to say, "Let's keep religion distant from the public square."

There is no necessary contradiction, Tipton argued, between biblical religion and a republican form of government. The republican notion of public life emphasizes that it is a continuing forum, a public discourse in which various views about public theology or public philosophy play their legitimate part. But in that discourse there has to be a kind of "translation" of language that enables everyone to take part—"not a translation from a religious to a secular vocabulary necessarily, but a process of dialectic that aims at sustaining civility—that is, at continuing the debate with those with whom we disagree." This approach also assumes a kind of polity that is neither "a purely minimalist state that overlooks a free market" nor a "scientific-bureaucratic state that regulates and administers the entire society." The church, said Tipton, cannot bless either of those understandings of the state. But the republic of continuing discourse also lays some obligations upon the church. To use the categories made famous by Ernst Troeltsch, the "church" side of the church must be strengthened against both the sectarian and mystical sides of the church. The sectarian says "To hell with the world. Withdraw from it. It has nothing to do with us." The mystical side, which ironically is the danger of the liberal churches, encourages a kind of radical individualism which is quite prepared to surrender to the state the task of "coordinating the whole society." And that direction can result in the state establishing some form of "civil religion," which is not what is called for in the republican idea of an ongoing argument and discourse.

Ed Hindson observed that fundamentalists have in the past failed to enter the argument as they should have. The outstanding instance of that was the civil rights movement.

HINDSON: We failed, utterly and totally. Only after it was finally over did we say, "Oh, that was a good thing. We're for that." We could have sped up the process, because our constituency certainly was part of what slowed it down. The concern of our people is not to fail again, for example on abortion.

Ed Dobson added that the right still has much to learn about the kind of republican discourse Neuhaus and Tipton were urging.

DOBSON: Although the religious right does have its fanatics and its extremists, hopefully we hold certain values because of our own private religious convictions which obviously are not going to change. But when we transfer those values into the public arena they should be, though they have not always been, transferred into some structure of civility, whereby even those who disagree with us are not seen to be anti-God or proponents of Satan or whatever you'd want to call them. As fundamentalists we can operate in that arena of civility whereby after the discussion and after the votes are counted we can go on living together as fellow human beings.

Mark Noll, historian that he is, described how our situation today is very different from that of, say, the nineteenth century. Then there was a "taken-for-grantedness about shared public values"; it persisted up to the time of John Dewey, but then it began to fall apart. Now it is evident that nobody can claim that their moral values are "obviously" normative for the culture. So the challenge today is different.

NOLL: What we need is to be instructed that it is necessary to translate our private beliefs into some kind of civil discourse. Built into that assertion is the assumption that that process of translation is necessary. Positivists do not believe that that translation process is necessary, because positivists know that simple, right-thinking people automatically see the value of a kind of technique. Protestants in the nineteenth century knew that you didn't have to translate, because all right-thinking people understood what moral value is like. But now we're in a situation where we must make that translation. One way of facilitating this would be to attack the myth of a neutral, secular anything. Secular methodologies do lead to secular worldviews. So it is important to suggest that no methodologies are, in principle, neutral. All things, science as much as anything, come from a human standpoint, a human community. No values can automatically be taken for granted in public. What is disastrous in the public arena is the belief that some values do not have to be translated into a form of civil discourse. In a genuinely pluralistic society, if people don't agree that they have to translate their private values into public discourse, then we are in Northern Ireland or Lebanon.

Robert Wuthnow observed that we are witnessing some curious switches in the parts played by different sectors of American religion.

WUTHNOW: Jerry Falwell is doing exactly what Neuhaus is suggesting. He's not bringing his church into the public square; he has formally differentiated Thomas Road Baptist Church from the Moral Majority. But he is bringing religious values into the public square. I would say there have been some serious negative repercussions from that, some costs as well as whatever benefits you may see. Some of those costs may be something as mundane as a loss of members. It may well be that one of the reasons fundamentalism has grown in America is that for fifty years fundamentalists stayed religiously out of the public sphere. And while the mainstream churches were taking the brunt of issues of justice and peace and the civil rights movement and the Vietnam conflict and so forth, these groups were staying out of it. Staying safe, so to speak.

One other negative implication may be the polarization that we see pretty strongly in American Christianity today. In a sense it's not simply a theological conflict, but it's now a political conflict. It may be that anytime that churches enter, directly or indirectly, the public sphere, they run the danger of exacerbating some of those conflicts. Or another possible cost may be that norms are picked up from the polity. So it isn't just religion infusing the polity, but the polity starts to change religion. Moral propositions may end up becoming mere preferences.

Midge Decter said she has been depressed by the ways in which religious groups seem to believe that the thing that really matters is political influence or "social change." Doesn't such a preoccupation with worldly power really betray a loss of faith in anything greater that the churches profess to believe?

Neuhaus agreed that engagement in the public square can lead to a "devious and devastating" belief that religion is somehow authenticated by its influence in the public square. If religion is to make a distinctive contribution to democratic politics, he urged, it must, among other things, sharply check the imperious notion of the all-importance of politics. Historically, he noted, the Roman Catholic Church was most criticized for its political ambitions.

NEUHAUS: When John Paul I was installed, the most remarkable thing was that he was *installed*. He was not crowned. He did not receive the papal tiara, which since the Middle Ages all popes have worn, which signified among other things terrestrial or temporal power. And when John Paul II was installed, he followed that precedent. The papacy has laid aside the tiara. I think this is one of the most powerful, symbolic statements. And I don't think that tiara will ever be put back on again. Unfortunately, a lot of other religious groups including the religious new right but also including, say, the United Methodist Church and the United Church of Christ, are all still wearing their pathetic little tiaras. They're all still trying to demonstrate influence as the world measures influence, and thereby compromising themselves very severely. Only a church that knows that it is vindicated only by the Word of God and ultimately vindicated by nothing other than the vindication of that Word in the coming of the messianic age and the fulfillment of the cosmic promise—only such a church can be useful in its culture-formation.

There was ready agreement around the table that it is never easy to sort out the transcendent and ultimate from the political and penultimate. "In a perhaps surprising way," Neuhaus said, "religion's engagement in the public discourse can help preserve the integrity of religion itself." That is, he continued, through such public engagement the church encounters truth claims that are both true and important, and it is thus held accountable to a discourse other than the discourse of its own confined religious world. "Without such engagement, any religious community can very easily become fanatical. The very word *fanatic* comes from the Latin *fanum*, which means 'to be inside the temple,' where there are no doors and there are no windows and there is no communication with anything outside the temple."

Wuthnow questioned whether the discussion was not assuming a distinction between "the religious" and "the public" that is not warranted. He suggested that the state is in fact changing and becoming, in some ways, more of a religion.

WUTHNOW: Democracy has been changing. The state has expanded its functions. Real income has doubled since World War II, but the growth of the state has been far greater than double since World War II. We need to think about the role of the public schools as an establishment with interests in their own right and about the growth of higher education as a secular establishment, heavily supported by the federal government. We need to think of the juvenile justice system or the courts or the expansion of the executive branch. I wonder if all of those things may be changing the reality or the character of American democracy enough so that as we rethink this issue of the relation between religion and democracy we need to think how religion can again revitalize and influence our understanding of the state.

Also, religion might protect us from this crisis of exceptionalism that may head us toward greater reliance on a technological myth or a pragmatic myth.

Paul Johnson agreed that today's problems result in large part from the fact that the state has become a quite different reality.

JOHNSON: One of the reasons why Americans in the nineteenth century didn't have this feeling of conflict between religion and the state was precisely because the state was so small. But of course once the state begins to take on all kinds of responsibilities, particularly in the role of social welfare, then it increasingly does tend to get involved in ethical disputes with very large numbers of constituents. One has to remember that the concept of welfare is religious. It started in the Diaspora, in the three centuries immediately before Christ, where the Jews operated a kind of miniature welfare state. Because the Christian religion grew up in the Jewish Diaspora, early Christians took on this work themselves and continued it throughout the Middle Ages. The only welfare available until the growth of the modern welfare state was essentially religious-based welfare. So the state has taken over the role of religion in welfare. And necessarily it began to operate its provision of welfare according to its own bureaucratic rules. Sooner or later, ethical conflicts with Christian believers are inevitable. That is what is happening. It didn't happen in the nineteenth century because the state wasn't that large.

We should be prepared to entertain and explore a very strong proposition, Neuhaus suggested—namely, that "God is on the side of democracy." Not necessarily any one historical form or even any one concept of democracy, and certainly not the very imperfect democracy that is America, he added. But while every historical moment is provisional and clearly falls short of the coming kingdom of God, Neuhaus said, "there is a remarkable fit between some basic biblical truth claims and the claims that undergird democratic governance." In terms of what are called "goods" in society, he said, "the single most important thing" is religious freedom. It might be argued that biblical obedience is the single most important thing, he acknowledged, but the meaning of biblical obedience can be determined only in a situation of religious freedom. In addition, if one believes that biblical obedience certainly means reverence for others as children of

God, then obedience requires protecting religious freedom also for those with whom we disagree about the meaning of biblical obedience. Given this priority of religious freedom, Neuhaus said, it follows that it is a matter of considerable importance to Christians that in today's world religious freedom be protected, even if only imperfectly, only in those societies that approximate what we call the democratic idea.

The Anatomy of a Crisis

"It strikes me," said Os Guiness, "that there is a real division in this room between those who think there is a real crisis about religion and democracy in America and those who don't." Maybe there had been a crisis, responded Theodore Caplow, and maybe there still was, but it was also possible that we're moving away from it. He noted that twenty years ago the college-educated population was distinctly less religious than other Americans, but "this is no longer the case. There are indications that it has been tipping the other way. . . . You can hardly call something a crisis when the phenomenon seems to be diminishing." The phenomenon in question, Caplow went on to say, is the sharp difference between the elite and the general population with respect to basic values. Others pointed out that the apparent change in the college-educated population is in part due to the fact that more people go to college, and so the distinction between the general public and the college-educated is no longer so important. In any case, it was agreed that the change that Caplow and others had detected will take a while to have its effect, since today's elite is from that earlier and less religious college population.

Allan Carlson of the Rockford Institute expressed some skepticism about research data that suggest major changes in the "religiousness" of the American people. He suggested that it is more accurate to stress continuities with the ways in which people go to church, say their prayers, and succumb to temptations that contradict all that they say they believe. The new thing, Carlson maintained, is indeed a matter of the elite who no longer consider themselves obligated to be guardians and transmitters of a social-moral vision. This, he said, is certainly true of the mainline Protestant clergy, who have in general been secularized, if by "secularized" we mean assimilated into the vision of societal leaders who are either indifferent or hostile to distinctively religious truth. "What I'm getting at is that the rot sets in at the top," said Carlson. "It is the failure of our elite communities to perpetuate both a vision of a moral social order and the will or the ability to defend it which may be the source of our problem."

Perhaps the question is not whether the college-educated or anyone else is more religious or less religious, says Robert Wuthnow. The question, rather, is what kind of religious content and style people are committed to. He urged that Marsden's distinction between theistic secularists and nontheistic secularists is one among several useful distinctions that need to be made. He also cited a recent study by Gallup on those who say they are "liberal religiously" and others who say they are "conservative religiously." Here, he noted, is where you get the really extreme differences, differences that pretty much reflect the polarization between "liberal" and "conservative" in every other area of society. Marsden strongly agreed, saying that "the struggle over who shapes the public philosophy is a struggle between people of quite different religious visions, and doesn't fit into a nice correlation of religion and morality, on the one hand, and irreligion and immorality, on the other." Similarly, said Marsden, the group is overplaying the elite/non-elite dichotomy; the real dichotomy is between competing moral traditions. Others joined in to point out that while the dichotomy may be between competing moral traditions, there is a strongly documented affinity of a "new class" elite for a moral tradition other than that embraced by the general population.

One problem, said Neuhaus, is that we are not always candid in acknowledging that the position we are taking is a moral position. We have people claiming they are value-free when asserting claims of obvious moral judgment. But a twin problem is that it is sometimes suggested that when we say something is a "moral issue" we are simply saying it is not open to public deliberation.

NEUHAUS: Today saying something is a moral issue simply means you turn up the volume. That's what moral issue has often come to mean in our politics. It's an issue on which you turn up the volume. For example, during the Vietnam War we heard many, many politicians say, "This is no longer a political issue. It's a *moral issue!*" What a dumb thing to say. As if politics were not moral. As though morality were not something to be debated and discussed.

George Gallup returned our attention to the dramatic differences between those who say they are religiously conservative and those who claim to be religiously liberal. Everett Ladd did not dispute the evidence on this score, but he wondered why some people find such polarizations so surprising or troubling. "In a highly participant society such as ours," he said, "of course you're going to have people sorting themselves out into camps." There may be no cause for alarm, others observed, so long as they aren't sorting themselves into armed camps. But, said Peter Berger, that's precisely the point.

BERGER: There is an empirical question: Are, in fact, these religiously based symbol systems necessary to keep a modern society together? What I find amazing is that listening to some of you around the table, one would expect this society to be in a state of armed conflict—with machine guns mowing down opponents. It is not! That raises an interesting question. Could it be that we exaggerate the importance of these common symbols? Could it be that at least modern societies seem to be able to function without that degree of legitimation, to use a sociological term? I do not know.

Maybe we don't need those common symbols as much as we thought, Midge Decter acknowledged, but she was not at all sure. A unique kind of civic harmony has been created in this country, she said.

DECTER: No other society has had to meld together so many groups of different cultural backgrounds. Part of the difficulty right now is that we do not have this consensus on absolutely fundamental questions. It is necessary for me as Jew and you as a Protestant to find a neutral territory, which is our public-civic life together, in which each of us leaves something at home, and we can live together without offering one another offense. Part of the difficulty at this moment is that there is offense being offered people all the time in the public square.

Decter acknowledged that there is still a degree of rhetorical consensus, but she maintained that it quickly falls apart when it comes to issues such as abortion, the role of religion in public schools, or what we ought to be teaching our children about sex and family life. "I think something pretty major has happened," she said, "when it is obvious, as it now is obvious, that we can no longer trust one another to draw up a syllabus for teaching about family life."

Several participants indicated that the reason we no longer trust one another is that we are no longer sure who the "we" is. The "we" is too often seen as the "them" of the bureaucratic state, especially in the case of the government monopoly on education. In addition, Caplow urged the group to recognize the "amazing" ways in which many of our moral problems are produced by well-intentioned but badly designed governmental programs. For example, the fact that more than eighty percent of black children in some of our cities are born out of wedlock is a result, in no small part, of "the government bounty offered for illegitimate births" through the current welfare system. So it's not simply that there has been a decline of civic trust or a general decline of morality but that governmental decisions made for good and moral reasons encourage patterns of behavior that nobody intended.

Diane Ravitch has spent her whole professional life working with public education and, in keeping with Caplow's point, she wanted us to understand the dilemma in which public education finds itself.

RAVITCH: One of the key problems that public schools have had in recent years is the public sense or perception that they have no values. It is impossible, goes the argument, in a pluralistic society for the public schools to have values because that would make them partisan, and they must be nonpartisan and secular. And so what has come in place of strong value orientation is values clarification. This becomes clear in the area of sex education. I reviewed last year the leading textbooks in this area, and they essentially say there is no right or wrong—it's what feels good, what feels right for you; if it's right for you, it's right. This probably explains a great deal of the expansion of private schooling, because of the search that many people have for some sense of right and wrong. The public schools in fact have given up any claim to an ultimate standard of right or wrong. Students, in effect, are in the naked public square with teachers acting as public officials and having no recourse to a standard of right and wrong.

Illustrating the truth of Ravitch's observation, Neuhaus told how in New York the city's leading newspaper editorially blasted the critics of a proposed sex education and family living curriculum. The critics had urged that the last thing that children who are the victims of family devastation needed to hear is that

the American family is "changing," that "family" no longer has
a normative meaning, that any association that provides caring
and satisfaction is a family, and so forth. Supporting the proposed
curriculum, the editorial writer asserted that the critics wanted
the schools to inculcate morality, which is not the business of
public schools. More ominously, according to the editorial, such
a normative approach would embarrass children who do not come
from stable families with a mother and a father in the home. The
moral imperative, it would seem, is not to embarrass anyone. But
this, observed Neuhaus, closes off any discussion in the public
arena of how things "ought to be." And that, several participants
noted, may well be the inevitable consequence of the dilemma
of public education described by Diane Ravitch.

There has been a far-reaching set of changes in the theoretical underpinnings of democratic society, Michael Novak said,
citing the earlier vision of Jacques Maritain.

NOVAK: Maritain is one of the thinkers who saw this most
clearly. He argued that we mustn't confuse the end of Christendom with secularization. We must see that there is also the
process of building up a new form of Christian humanism of a
different shape than before. He framed the issue in this way. We
long thought that societies needed a theoretic creed, they needed
a legitimation structure which gave them a view of reality and
a consensus about that. He thought that a distinctive difference
in the American type society is that it has found a way of living
on a practical creed, a consensus about values in the human
person to be respected in practice. Now, to be sure, he saw clearly
enough that this depended on a theoretic creed of several different
sorts. Its required respect for the person meant that you resolve
issues by civil argument, for example.

But now, said Novak, we've reached the point where the
practical creed seems to be breaking down because we can no
longer ignore its theoretical underpinnings. And, when we do
examine those underpinnings, we discover that not only do we
not agree about them but also that we don't know how to debate
our disagreements in a democratic manner.

Novak cited examples of great changes that have taken
place in the past twenty years or so. Once we talked about tolerance, but now, he said, tolerance has been redefined as relativism.
Once we talked about diversity in the public square, but that has
been turned into emptying the public square of discourse about

the things on which we most significantly differ. We have gone, Novak argued, from nondiscrimination to an enforcement of non-discrimination, which inevitably requires new discriminations. Most seriously, we have in almost every area "moved from language about moral conviction to language about preference." In an aside, Novak suggested that the most obvious issue that demonstrates these changes is not abortion but homosexuality, "a question not as often talked about for fear of embarrassing somebody." In any event, said Novak, we can agree that the founders were wise in trying to devise a system that involved the polity as little as possible in debate over presuppositions. But if we are to be as wise today, we will have to recognize that the presuppositions they thought could be taken for granted are no longer in place. "There can be a commons, or a public square, that is empty in the sense of not having established beliefs about presuppositions, but it must at least be filled with the sound of argument." Impassioned warfare between people of conflicting "preferences" is not the kind of civil argument that Novak has in mind.

"What is change and what is crisis?" asked Stanley Rothman. "It's hard to sort it out." But his hunch was that change has reached crisis proportions when large segments of the population "are no longer sure about the basic rightness of American culture and what we are vaguely aware of as its religious underpinnings." Berger, half apologetically, brought us back to the question of the elite. He had been struck by Midge Decter's account of how it used to be in intergroup relations, symbolized by the rabbi-minister-priest on the public stage. It had been suggested that that was a hypocritical period in American life that has now been exposed, but Berger questioned that.

BERGER: We're talking about a twenty-year period. It didn't happen before 1945. It presumably did not last beyond 1965. So we're dealing with a twenty-year moment in American history. It happened to be the period in which I came to America from Europe, and I didn't at all have the feeling that this was hypocritical. On the contrary, the main thing that struck me—and I know I was not alone—is how similar all these people were. Protestants, Catholics, Jews—they all seemed to be very similar. Then something happened in the 1960s. There are at least two very different interpretations one could have of it. One can say how hypocritical all this was, and then the hypocrisy was revealed. But is there not another interpretation? Which is not that hypocrisy was revealed but that a particular small segment of the population (and here we're back to the cultural elite) took a very different value stance and a conflict erupted between that group and the common mass of the population. I am inclined to hold the second.

Novak invited us to reflect on whether there is not some strange overlap between hypocrisy and reality. He told about a meeting in the 1950s, between Protestant, Catholic, and Jewish leaders sponsored by the Fund for the Republic. Notables such as Father John Courtney Murray and John Cogley, a leading Catholic layman, were involved. During the day everything was cordial and civil, but later, over drinks, the conviction was expressed by many participants that one could not *really* be fully part of the American republic and also a serious Roman Catholic.

NOVAK: It seems to me, that such a meeting represented a certain hypocrisy and certain reality, and it's hard to sort them out. The reality came out over drinks, and then was brought back into conversation with what was said earlier. What was said earlier may have been hypocrisy, or maybe it should be viewed as a realistic statement of how people thought things ought to be. In any event, not long after, a Catholic was elected president.

You may not want to call it hypocrisy, Ed Hindson observed, but there was, from a fundamentalist viewpoint, something unreal about the way the stage used to be set.

HINDSON: When you put the Protestant, the Catholic, and the Jew up there, the fundamentalists sat there and said, "We're not represented. We're not any one of those three. We are not represented by the liberal Protestant. So we don't have representation." So we saw through the hypocrisy of that immediately. That never impressed our people.

Dean Kelley of the National Council of Churches, one of the most astute analysts of religion in America, agreed that the fundamentalists had been excluded.

KELLEY: For fifty years or more the fundamentalist leadership was "pariah-ized" by the religious elite of the Protestant world. The ministerial association never dreamed of inviting that clod from the Assemblies of God or the Independent Baptist Church or whatever because he really didn't belong. So, the mainline churches are getting some of that back now. We earned it very well.

But on another question posed by fundamentalists and others, concerning the dangers of secularization, Kelley had misgivings.

KELLEY: I have been trying to resort to the New Testament to see if it entertains the category of secularization, and if it does, whether it views it as a threat. And I don't recall finding it there, certainly not as a threat. Certainly Christians lived in an almost totally non-Christian culture. And yet today many Christians speak of secularization as a great peril or threat or problem. But in the New Testament the problems, the threats to the faith, were not those who did not themselves entertain the faith, or perhaps even so much those that persecuted it, as the categories of idolatry and unfaithfulness. That is, the failures of the faithful were the real threats to the faith, not the indifference or even the hostility of the outsiders. So I wonder where from a New Testament source you derive the mandate of Christianity for feeling threatened by secularization.

Brian Benestad agreed that the problem is the failure of the faithful and cited an example from contemporary Catholicism.

BENESTAD: We Roman Catholics have lost some things. In the realm of catechetics, for example. I live in a town of five thousand people. I went to the local church to hear a lecture that was given to parents whose kids were going to receive first communion. A third grade teacher got up and started talking about values clarification and stages of development. They would move from heteronomy to autonomy, and that would be the highest level of Christian living. Fortunately, most of the parents fell asleep. It is a problem: catechetics has been overwhelmed by this shallow understanding of Christianity. These are cultural elite at a lower level of the cultural elite dictating what's in the catechism. It's going to be very difficult to have a public philosophy if we don't really have a sound grip on our own tradition.

Lest anyone be left with the impression that the failure of the faithful is not a problem among fundamentalists, Ed Dobson wanted to set the record straight.

DOBSON: There is a breakdown in theological preaching— not in the public square but in our faith communities. For example, preaching about sin twenty years ago in the pulpits of our various faith communities was dramatically different than what we want to preach today. Is that a contributing factor to the breakdown of what we consider the morals within society? Even within the fundamentalist community we hesitate to preach on hell now. We believe in it, but it's really not palatable. I'm not saying that we don't preach on it, but there's that tendency. That may be one of the contributing factors that suggests why so many people are religious and so few committed. Because we're not preaching that kind of commitment and from our pulpits we are reducing the demands of our discipleship.

It's fine to emphasize the importance of the faithful being faithful, Steven Tipton acknowledged, but along that way can also lie a temptation to sectarianism.

TIPTON: We end up thinking that the only really moral communities are these small, voluntary associations of deep commitment and organic relationship. Then the larger society is viewed as a huge and neutral associational sea in which these communities float. Meaningful moral argument is limited to these small communities.

The result is that those outside communities are quite willing to tolerate them so long as everyone agrees that their claims about the gospel are nothing more than opinions, Tipton suggested. "The viewpoint is that X, Y, or Z happen to believe such and such, but there's no reason why the rest of us have to take them seriously." But then X or Y want something changed in the larger society, and because they can't really converse, can't really argue with anyone outside their community, they engage not in conversation but in lobbying. "The result is the worst kind of politics— the politics of pure power—and that is the result we're already witnessing today."

Well yes, said Caplow, but X or Y might not feel the urge to change things in the area of government if government had not so vastly expanded its province over the past fifty years. "We are increasingly confronted," Caplow said, "with the clumsy and murderous state, which has somehow evolved out of our republic. And that is what has produced moral problems that did not seem to be there before."

Carlson developed this point, suggesting that what are often seen as the problems of religion, modernization, secularization, and so forth, may be, at least in large part, problems created by some wrongheaded people making bad decisions.

CARLSON: A good share of our difficulty derives from the portentous decision of a small group of federal judges to nationalize moral questions in a way that was never done before the middle decades of this century. There is no doubt that if the federal courts had not drawn *Roe v. Wade* up to the Supreme Court and that decision had never been made, the abortion debate would have gone in a very different way. And I would suspect that the polarization we see would not have happened— at least to the same degree. It would have been a far more localized, a far more complicated arrangement. The same could be said on school prayer, the decisions on religious symbols in public places, and so on. Again, there was no historical inevitability that the Supreme Court had to decide as it did.

The role of the courts is critical, Caplow agreed, in "circumventing" the democratic process. He cited examples of how people "put up with" public policy decisions that went against their wishes when the decision was made through public debate and the ballot box. "Presumably we have enough civility so we can put up with moral decisions that go against us, provided they go against us by the prescribed route of majority rule. Otherwise, we begin objecting, and civility begins to shake a bit."

If there is a crisis, Ernest Fortin urged, it is a crisis of the mind: "The kinds of things we're talking about, they don't affect so much the people on the street out there. These things come and go. They don't necessarily affect the flow of history." The crisis, he suggested, is not so much that democracy isn't working in an everyday sort of way but that so few people are convinced democrats, able to make a convincing case for democracy. The last really able defense of democracy, says Fortin, was that of John Stuart Mill, well over a century ago.

FORTIN: All the things we've been talking about—values clarification, values neutrality, cultural relativism, ethical relativism—they're all powerful forces. They're not diminishing, and I suspect we've yet to see their full impact. I don't know what, if anything, we can do to stop them, but perhaps the most important thing is to develop alternatives, including making the case for democracy in a new way.

In the religious community almost nobody is making the case for democracy, Neuhaus noted, at least not in a theologically serious way. The moral majoritarians aren't, at least not yet. And they still have to contend with theocrats—or "theonomists" as they call themselves—who think of democracy as a temporary expedient to be exploited until "the dominion of Bible law-order is established." Much of the religious left and theological education is "into" liberation theology, which is generally vociferous in its opposition to liberal democracy. As for the moderate and mainline, Neuhaus recalled a conversation in which he tried at length to persuade an editor of the moral status of democracy and religious freedom. "Richard, I don't understand you," the editor said. "I don't understand why you're so insistent. I agree with you. I like democracy. I'm all in favor of religious freedom. These are my values. I'm just saying that there's nothing universal about them." The reason he thinks there is nothing universal about them, Neuhaus argued, is that he assumes they are not true in any philosophically serious sense of the term. The democratic idea is an accident of one's historical placement, a matter of "cultural conditioning," not a truth about the ordering of human relationships for which one ought to contend.

The Sect, the Church, and the Republic

George Marsden urged that the truth of the Republic and of the democratic idea needs to be held in tension with Christian commitment.

MARSDEN: Are the secularists a threat to the Republic? Are they a threat to Christianity? The second of those questions is, from my perspective, much more interesting than the first. I consider the first to be important; that is, I am interested in the future of the Republic, and I like the Republic, and I don't know anything better, and I hope for its preservation and am willing to work for that. But if it came to a choice between saving the Republic and corrupting or diluting Christianity, then it seems to me the Republic would have to go on my set of priorities. So I see my calling as a Christian historian to be looking to try to separate the gold from the dross, to try to peel away the accidental cultural developments that have been taken to be the central, authentic parts of the Christian tradition and try to get back toward the purer thing, whatever that is.

This kicked off a lively discussion of whether Marsden had posed the right choices. Does God have intentions in history beyond the history of the church? Might it be that, however imperfectly perceived by us, there are divine intentions engaged also in the political struggles of our time? Marsden expressed worry about political systems that think they have "God on their side," suggesting that they tend to turn into Northern Irelands and Lebanons. But, several participants suggested that perhaps something like the "resacralization of democracy" could strengthen the democratic check on such doleful possibilities. Marsden's way of putting the issue clearly moved the discussion deeper into ways of thinking about the community of faith—whether in terms of sectarian, churchly, or mystical models.

It was observed that some very serious thinkers today are moving in an unapologetically sectarian direction. Their message is that the public arena is now clearly dominated by barbarians to whom reasoned moral discourse is completely alien. Therefore, say those who follow the line of argument in Alasdair MacIntyre's *After Virtue*, the only thing to do is to find whatever residual moral communities one can and hole up there for the duration. "I can understand and sympathize with the sectarian alternative," said Neuhaus, "but my argument is that it is the greater act of courage, the greater venture of faith, to enter into the public history of one's time." We are responsible to God, he suggested, not only for our membership in the church but also in other communities, including that "community" called America. And if the idea of democracy that that community helps to keep alive in the world is good for people, then participation in this political experiment can be seen as part of one's obedience to the command to love our neighbors. So, according to this view, we do not have to choose between authentic Christianity and the Republic.

Tipton reminded the group of the ways in which sectarianism gave historical birth to ideas central to democracy. Still today, he insisted, sectarianism, by its very fidelity to its own vision, can be an agent of renewal in society.

TIPTON: But the key thing really is moral exemplification. You don't just mouth the gospel, or what the professional clergy tells you is the gospel, but you seek to live it out. Moral exemplification not only by religious groups but by 'moral associations,' as Tocqueville calls them, is absolutely essential to the argument of civic life. We need to see people trying to live it out. And that is part of the ongoing experiment, not just of the society as a whole but of groups in it. It's not either/or. It's not sect to the exclusion of church or church to the exclusion of sect.

But according to Dean Kelley one does not have enough time or energy to do something about everything. Choices must be made, or at least priorities set.

KELLEY: I have to go with the sect type, as opposed to the church type, purely on the basis of relative energy levels. The sect came in for a few denigrations yesterday. We characterized the sect type in two perjorative ways: isolation and aggressive outreach, neither very lovely traits. We left out the "energistic center," which is the genius of the sect type, which in the early stage of the evolution of a religious movement is neither isolation nor aggression but embodiment. The new movement, being small, is not able to have a massive effect on the culture in an umbrella or overarching way. But by being able to command very high levels of commitment and energy among its few adherents, it can have a far more penetrating effect by embodying the new concept of how human life ought to be lived. Those are the kinds of things that have shaped societies in the Western tradition, including the Wesleyan evangelical forces and the Cromwellian Puritan forces in England, which had far more effect on England than centuries of the established church, because they had a higher energy level.

Yes, Ralph Potter of Harvard agreed, each of us has to make some choices. But our choices do not necessarily entail that those who choose differently are wrong.

POTTER: To be a good Troelschian you have to say, "I am a sectarian" or "I am a church-type" or "I am a mystical-type." But I know the fullness of the gospel is served only when there are these counterbalancing forces which reassert the elements that I neglect—in effect because of my human finitude, my inability to comprehend and express all that's going on. I am one or another of these forms of Christian expression, but I've got to rejoice that there are these other types so that when I stretch too far the pattern of Christian faith, they push me back toward a more appropriate pattern.

As will become evident, others were more insistent upon the need to say that some choices are wrong, that some choices made by others debase the shared context in which all of us must do our choosing.

To Think Anew

When American religion has sometimes seemed most vital it has also seemed least intellectually compelling, said Michael Novak. The Catholic tradition is a tradition of intellect, but in America it has usually lived far below its tradition in that respect.

NOVAK: What we all see, whether hopefully or despairing-
ly, as a very new moment in American life requires a deepening
of religion, and deepening that centers more on the mind, so that
we can really make an argument in public. . . . I take much of the
ferment in the evangelical and fundamentalist communities to be
a movement toward a theology. That is, for the first time a critical
mass of fundamentalist and evangelical Christians are college-
educated and graduate-school-educated, and they're facing questions which did not occur on the frontier, when they were all
standing over against the poorhouse crowd and the country club
set. You see more and more explorations today: Does Christianity mean this, does it mean that, how does it relate to this work,
how does it relate to that tradition, how do evangelical understandings relate to Catholic ones? There is the beginning of a
theology. I think we really need to press that on all fronts if we
are to speak to the public philosophy.

There was a consensus that, in important respects, America
is now challenged to become a pluralistic society for the first
time. The problem is that we have sects militantly pushing their
wares in the public square, and because their pushing is not
accompanied by moral argument, it appears that their wares are
nothing more than preferences. The question, said Neuhaus, is
"How do we move toward genuine democratic pluralism in which
we turn preferences and propositions into the stuff of persuasion
and public discourse?" Tipton agreed, noting that "it is not a
moral argument to say that X outrages me or that Y is a moral
outrage. It becomes a moral argument when I respond to an
interlocutor's questions about why I say something is wrong and
by what authority. And then my response has to be more than
simply *my* assertion; it has to be placed within an ongoing dia-
logue, a tradition of reason-giving and disputation. In short, real
pluralism requires an encounter of traditions." With other participants, Tipton contended that what has too often been called
pluralism has been in fact a studied evasion of such encounter.

Encounter, Neuhaus claimed, also means ecumenism. At
this point he took gentle issue with some of Paul Johnson's earlier
negative assertions about the ecumenical movement. "Ecumenism that is authentic, that does not evade but engages differences,
aims at demonstrating to the world a religious basis for the human
hope for unity. That basis was largely destroyed in the sixteenth
and seventeenth centuries by the wars of religion, which led
many people to pursue the hope for human unity in all kinds of

ill-fated political utopias," he said. But he strongly affirmed what Johnson said about the linkage between specific traditions and a sense of being accountable. In more general terms, Johnson underlined the importance of the notion of accountability, or judgment, itself:

> JOHNSON: People may not like the idea of hell—or indeed believe in it anymore—but I think people like to be judged. I think there is a deep desire in most of us that our life should not be regarded as insignificant, that there should be some outside supreme power who will pass a verdict on our life. That is why I think so many people believe in an afterlife and they believe in a judgment—because they want to be judged. They want to be treated with the respect inherent in the fact that they are worth judging. So although hell as a force for fear may disappear, I think the sense that we are coming up to trial at some stage and that a verdict is going to be passed on us is very deep-rooted in human beings and is very precious.

That understanding of judgment, it was noted, can be related to the value of America's having put the phrase "under God" into the Pledge of Allegiance in 1954, despite the questionable reasons for having done so. And that led to some reflections on patriotism.

> JOHNSON: Dr. Johnson once said that patriotism is the last refuge of a scoundrel. That saying is often misunderstood. What he meant by that is that there are two forms of devotion to your country. One was the old form, which had the divine sanction, in which you saw the monarch as the embodiment of the country. The monarch was the father of the country. In the sense that the head of the family was in charge of the family, the monarch was in charge of the national family. That was the true, old-fashioned, divinely sanctioned devotion to your country. Now opposed to that was the notion that the country itself is the *patria*, the country itself is the father. Dr. Johnson in his wonderfully penetrating way saw the dangers of this. He saw the new form of patriotism leading to the monster state, in which the state took over, the state was the father, the state was the thing which pushed everyone around. And that is why he disliked this new form of patriotism and could see that it would attract a scoundrel. And of course what is the twentieth century but a history of scoundrelism working through the state?

Ed Dobson confessed himself very attracted to the ways in which some participants had attempted to rearticulate the connections between being faithful and being American. But he was not entirely convinced that this does not pose a threat to the vitality of fundamentalism.

DOBSON: There is within fundamentalism at least some attempt to come back to the intellectual dimension. But I see two great risks in that. The one risk is that in our quest for intellectual respectability or credibility, our attempt to sit with the intellectual elite or whatever, our propositions within that process would be reduced to preferences. They would then no longer be meaningful for any type of public discussion. The second concern is that within the context of becoming perhaps more intellectual in our approach to issues that we end up speaking to the elite, for the elite, and end up as a voice crying in the wilderness with few listening. I am concerned that whenever we address an issue, we address it for the common man. Because fundamentalists care very little what the intellectual elite think on anything. I am concerned that we don't lose our contact with the common man who is at the heart and soul of our movement.

To Dobson's concern, one conferee urged that fundamentalists, and everyone else for that matter, should not be excessively concerned about whether they're speaking for millions or for a handful, whether what they say is demonstrably effective or spoken into the air (perhaps into the ear of God, and overheard by the saints?). "Effective truth is very nice, but truth is the important part. If it's effective, that's a plus," said Neuhaus.

After the conference was over, George Marsden offered some summary ruminations that can perhaps serve as the last word, at least this time around. Is there a crisis? "I agree there is a crisis; but historically it's clear that this can be said of virtually every era, and theologically it's just what I would expect in the City of the World." Nonetheless, within the "realistic limits that I start out with," he declared himself an optimist. "It is important to think of the present as a time of opportunity." In all the swirling claims and counterclaims that pass as moral argument in America, Marsden senses that there may be a resource for the centering of a new kind of conversation. It may be found in looking again at the eighteenth-century "common sense" philosophies, a venerable tradition that has been contemptuously dismissed by positivists, historicists, and other absolutistic relativists.

Marsden notes that among the merits of this proposal is the fact that the common sense tradition is deeply rooted in America's founding period. It is also ecumenical in that there are affinities between common sense principles and the concepts of Catholic natural law, Calvinist common grace, and Lutheran two-kingdoms thought. But that, as Marsden concluded, may be the subject of another conference. It raises a cluster of interesting questions that naturally follow from this discussion, in which we moved from the massive facticity of "unsecular America" to the problems of articulating the sacred in a democratic and pluralistic public square.

Appendix

Facts and Figures on Unsecular America

Table 1
GALLUP CROSS-NATIONAL VALUES SURVEYS, 1981

In the long run, do you think that scientific advances we are making will help or harm mankind?

	Will help	Some of each	Will harm	Don't know
United States	58%	22%	16%	4%
Great Britain	48	26	22	4
Spain	44	31	18	7
Republic of Ireland	38	26	28	8
Italy	38	36	20	6
Northern Ireland	37	35	22	6
France	36	36	21	6
Finland	35	35	27	3
Sweden	34	41	21	4
West Germany	33	39	21	7
Norway	32	42	23	3
Denmark	31	42	20	7
Belgium	26	45	17	12
Netherlands	23	32	36	9

Which, if any, of the following do you belong to? Churches or religious organizations.

	Belong to churches or religious organizations
United States	57%
Northern Ireland	51
Netherlands	35
Republic of Ireland	31
Great Britain	22
Spain	15
West Germany	13
Norway	10
Belgium	9
Sweden	9
Finland	9
Italy	7
France	4
Denmark	4

Apart from weddings, funerals and baptisms, about how often do you attend religious services these days?

	Once a week or more	Once a month	Christmas, Easter, or other specific Holy Days	Once a year or less	Never/ practically never	Don't know
Republic of Ireland	82%	6%	4%	5%	4%	0%
Northern Ireland	52	15	7	14	11	0
United States	43	16	9	15	16	2
Spain	41	12	10	11	25	0
Italy	36	16	19	9	21	0
Netherlands	27	13	9	9	41	2
Belgium	30	8	10	18	34	1
West Germany	21	16	19	25	20	0
Great Britain	14	9	12	20	46	0
France	12	6	13	12	57	0
Norway	7	10	27	22	35	0
Sweden	5	8	12	34	41	0
Denmark	3	9	17	28	43	0

NOTE: Rank ordered by combined responses "once a week or more" and "once a month."

Which, if any, of the following do you belong to? And do you currently do any unpaid voluntary work for any of them? Churches or religious organizations.

	Do unpaid voluntary work for churches or religious organizations
United States	23%
Northern Ireland	14
Spain	10
Netherlands	9
Republic of Ireland	8
Great Britain	7
West Germany	7
Norway	6
Belgium	5
Italy	5
Sweden	5
Finland	4
France	3
Denmark	2

Generally speaking, do you think that your church is giving, in your country, adequate answers to . . . man's spiritual needs?

	Yes	No	Don't know
United States	73%	14%	13%
Republic of Ireland	64	24	12
Northern Ireland	60	24	15
Finland	58	21	21
Norway	50	28	22
France	48	37	15
West Germany	47	33	20
Spain	45	37	18
Italy	43	29	28
Great Britain	42	32	26
Belgium	40	29	31
Sweden	37	35	29
Netherlands	33	29	38
Denmark	26	45	29

Do you find that you get comfort and strength from religion or not?

	Yes	No	Don't know
United States	79%	17%	4%
Republic of Ireland	79	17	5
Northern Ireland	70	22	7
Italy	63	30	7
Spain	57	34	9
Belgium	47	32	20
Great Britain	46	49	5
West Germany	44	39	14
Netherlands	43	44	13
Norway	40	38	22
France	37	57	6
Denmark	29	60	11
Sweden	27	63	10

Do you take some moments of prayer, meditation or contemplation or something like that?

	Yes	No	Don't know
United States	85%	14%	1%
Republic of Ireland	81	18	1
Northern Ireland	73	25	1
Italy	72	26	2
Spain	69	27	4
Norway	61	38	1
West Germany	59	29	12
Belgium	56	32	12
Netherlands	56	36	8
Great Britain	50	50	0
Finland	49	42	10
Denmark	48	50	2
France	44	54	2
Sweden	33	66	2

Which, if any, of the following do you believe in?
  God

	Yes, believe	No, don't believe	Don't know
United States	95%	2%	3%
Republic of Ireland	95	3	2
Northern Ireland	91	3	5
Spain	87	8	6
Italy	84	10	6
Belgium	77	12	10
Great Britain	76	16	9
West Germany	72	16	12
Norway	72	22	7
Netherlands	65	25	10
France	62	29	9
Denmark	58	27	15
Sweden	52	35	14

Which, if any, of the following do you believe in?
  Heaven

	Yes, believe	No, don't believe	Don't know
United States	84%	11%	5%
Republic of Ireland	83	10	7
Northern Ireland	81	10	9
Great Britain	57	32	11
Spain	50	38	12
Norway	48	42	11
Finland	46	36	19
Italy	41	44	15
Netherlands	39	47	14
Belgium	33	45	22
West Germany	31	54	15
France	27	65	9
Sweden	26	59	14
Denmark	17	67	16

Which, if any, of the following do you believe in?
  Hell

	Yes, believe	No, don't believe	Don't know
United States	67%	26%	7%
Northern Ireland	65	21	14
Republic of Ireland	54	35	10
Spain	34	52	14
Italy	31	52	17
Great Britain	27	63	11
Finland	22	58	20
Norway	22	68	11
Belgium	18	60	23
Netherlands	15	71	14
France	15	77	8
West Germany	14	73	13
Sweden	10	80	10
Denmark	8	81	12

Which, if any, of the following do you believe in?
  Life after death

	Yes, believe	No, don't believe	Don't know
Republic of Ireland	76%	14%	11%
Northern Ireland	72	14	14
United States	71	17	13
Spain	55	26	18
Finland	49	32	20
Italy	47	33	19
Great Britain	45	35	19
Norway	44	40	16
Netherlands	42	40	18
West Germany	39	40	21
Belgium	37	39	24
France	35	50	14
Denmark	26	55	19

Which, if any, of the following do you believe in?
  The devil

	Yes, believe	No, don't believe	Don't know
Northern Ireland	66%	22%	12%
United States	66	28	7
Republic of Ireland	57	34	9
Spain	33	53	14
Italy	30	55	15
Great Britain	30	60	10
Finland	29	53	18
Norway	28	62	10
Belgium	20	59	21
Netherlands	20	66	14
West Germany	18	70	12
France	17	76	8
Denmark	12	77	11
Sweden	12	77	11

Which of these statements comes closest to your beliefs?
  There is a personal God.
  There is some sort of spirit or life force.
  I don't really know what to think.
  I don't really think there is any sort of spirit, God, or life force.

	There is a personal God	Some sort of spirit/ life force	I don't know what to think	I don't think there is spirit, God, or life force	Don't know
Rep. of Ireland	73%	16%	6%	2%	3%
Northern Ireland	70	18	8	1	3
United States	65	26	5	1	2
Spain	55	23	12	6	5
Norway	40	31	18	9	2
Belgium	39	24	15	8	14
Netherlands	34	29	17	12	8
Great Britain	31	39	19	9	3
Italy	26	50	11	6	6
France	26	26	22	19	7
Finland	25	45	12	6	11
West Germany	24	40	17	13	6
Denmark	24	24	22	21	10
Sweden	19	39	19	17	6

Here is a card on which are the Ten Commandments. Please look at them and tell me, for each one, whether it still applies fully today, whether it applies today to a limited extent, or no longer really applies today for yourself.

I am the Lord thy God, thou shalt have no other gods before me.

	Applies fully	Applies to limited extent	Doesn't apply	Don't know
Republic of Ireland	90%	11%	6%	3%
United States	79	10	8	3
Northern Ireland	75	15	9	1
Italy	68	12	17	3
Spain	48	28	19	5
Great Britain	48	21	29	2
Belgium	47	22	17	13
Norway	47	19	30	5
West Germany	45	17	26	12
Denmark	45	14	19	22
Finland	44	31	18	8
Netherlands	40	15	32	13
France	30	17	48	5
Sweden	30	14	48	9

Thou shalt not take the name of the Lord thy God in vain.

	Applies fully	Applies to limited extent	Doesn't apply	Don't know
United States	68%	20%	10%	2%
Italy	66	14	18	2
Northern Ireland	60	26	13	0
Republic of Ireland	56	27	14	3
Spain	52	26	17	5
Norway	50	25	21	3
West Germany	50	21	17	12
Netherlands	49	18	24	9
Great Britain	43	24	32	2
Belgium	42	24	20	14
Sweden	33	19	41	7
Finland	31	37	24	8
Denmark	29	34	23	15
France	24	18	52	5

Thou shalt keep the Sabbath holy.

	Applies fully	Applies to limited extent	Doesn't apply	Don't know
Republic of Ireland	68%	16%	13%	2%
United States	57	24	17	2
Northern Ireland	52	24	22	1
Italy	51	16	30	2
Spain	38	28	30	2
Norway	34	31	33	2
Belgium	33	24	31	12
West Germany	29	32	30	8
Finland	25	40	29	7
Great Britain	25	24	49	2
Netherlands	24	20	47	9
France	20	19	57	5
Sweden	16	19	61	4
Denmark	13	27	53	7

Thou shalt honor thy mother and thy father.

	Applies fully	Applies to limited extent	Doesn't apply	Don't know
Italy	91%	6%	2%	1%
United States	90	7	1	2
Northern Ireland	85	12	3	0
Great Britain	83	12	5	1
Republic of Ireland	77	13	8	3
Spain	75	16	5	4
Norway	73	18	6	2
Belgium	73	15	5	7
West Germany	72	23	2	3
Netherlands	69	20	5	6
France	67	19	10	4
Finland	65	24	4	7
Sweden	63	24	9	3
Denmark	62	25	5	8

Thou shalt not kill.

	Applies fully	Applies to limited extent	Doesn't apply	Don't know
Italy	96%	2%	2%	1%
United States	93	4	1	2
Republic of Ireland	93	4	2	2
Norway	93	3	2	2
Northern Ireland	92	6	2	0
Great Britain	90	6	3	1
Denmark	90	4	2	5
Sweden	90	4	4	2
West Germany	88	9	2	2
Netherlands	82	9	4	6
Spain	81	9	6	4
Belgium	80	9	6	6
France	80	9	8	4
Finland	79	10	5	6

Thou shalt not commit adultery.

	Applies fully	Applies to limited extent	Doesn't apply	Don't know
United States	87%	8%	3%	2%
Northern Ireland	86	9	4	1
Republic of Ireland	85	7	5	3
Great Britain	78	12	9	2
Sweden	70	15	10	5
Norway	69	21	7	2
Finland	67	19	7	7
Denmark	67	11	9	13
West Germany	64	22	8	5
Italy	62	14	21	2
Belgium	61	20	11	9
Spain	58	24	13	5
Netherlands	50	23	21	5
France	48	18	29	5

Thou shalt not steal.

	Applies fully	Applies to limited extent	Doesn't apply	Don't know
United States	93%	5%	1%	2%
Italy	93	4	2	1
Norway	92	4	2	2
Northern Ireland	91	7	2	0
Republic of Ireland	88	7	2	2
Sweden	88	5	4	3
Great Britain	87	8	4	1
Denmark	84	9	2	5
West Germany	81	14	2	2
Netherlands	79	12	6	4
Spain	78	11	7	4
Finland	78	10	6	6
Belgium	76	10	6	7
France	69	14	14	4

Thou shalt not bear false witness against thy neighbor.

	Applies fully	Applies to limited extent	Doesn't apply	Don't know
United States	89%	8%	1%	2%
Italy	88	7	4	1
Republic of Ireland	86	8	3	3
Northern Ireland	84	11	3	1
Sweden	84	8	5	4
Great Britain	78	14	5	3
Norway	75	20	3	2
Denmark	74	16	2	7
West Germany	73	20	4	4
France	67	16	13	4
Finland	61	27	6	6
Belgium	61	23	7	9
Netherlands	57	29	8	5
Spain	56	30	10	4

Thou shalt not covet thy neighbor's wife.

	Applies fully	Applies to limited extent	Doesn't apply	Don't know
United States	89%	6%	2%	2%
Republic of Ireland	85	8	3	3
Norway	80	13	4	2
Northern Ireland	79	17	3	1
Great Britain	79	9	10	3
Sweden	75	11	9	5
Denmark	72	16	4	9
Finland	65	21	7	7
Spain	65	20	11	5
Netherlands	65	17	13	6
Belgium	65	16	9	10
Italy	64	14	20	2
West Germany	62	24	8	7
France	52	18	25	5

Thou shalt not covet thy neighbor's goods.

	Applies fully	Applies to limited extent	Doesn't apply	Don't know
United States	88%	8%	2%	2%
Republic of Ireland	87	6	4	3
Northern Ireland	85	9	4	2
Norway	79	14	5	3
Great Britain	79	12	8	1
Italy	73	12	13	1
Denmark	72	15	4	9
Sweden	71	12	12	6
West Germany	70	20	4	6
Belgium	69	16	7	8
Finland	65	21	7	6
France	62	16	18	4
Spain	61	24	11	5
Netherlands	59	24	12	6

SOURCE: Surveys by the Gallup Organization and Gallup International Research Institute for the Center for Applied Research in the Apostolate and the European Values System Study Group, 1981.

Table 2
BELIEF IN GOD, HEAVEN, AND AN AFTER LIFE

Do you believe in a God?

	Yes	No
United States	98%	2%
Greece	96	2
Austria	85	10
Switzerland	84	11
Finland	83	7
West Germany	81	10
Netherlands	79	13
Great Britain	77	11
France	73	21
Norway	73	12
Sweden	60	26

Do you believe in Heaven?

	Yes	No	No opinion
United States	85%	11%	4%
Greece	65	23	12
Finland	62	20	18
Norway	60	20	20
Great Britain	54	27	19
Netherlands	54	31	15
Switzerland	50	41	9
Austria	44	49	7
Sweden	43	42	15
West Germany	43	42	15
France	39	52	9

Do you believe in life after death?

	Yes	No	No opinion
United States	73%	19%	8%
Greece	57	28	15
Finland	55	23	22
Norway	54	25	21
Netherlands	50	35	15
Switzerland	50	41	9
West Germany	41	45	14
Great Britain	38	35	27

SOURCE: Surveys by the Gallup Organization and Gallup International Research Institute, July 1968.

Table 3
CONFIDENCE IN INSTITUTIONS

Percent saying "great deal" or "quite a lot" combined

	1984	1983	1981	1979	1977	1975	1973
Church or organized religion	64%	62%	64%	65%	64%	68%	66%
Military	58	53	50	54	57	58	NA
Banks and banking	51	51	46	60	NA	NA	NA
U.S. Supreme Court	51	42	46	45	46	49	44
Public schools	47	39	42	53	54	NA	58
Newspapers	34	38	35	51	NA	NA	39
Organized labor	30	26	28	36	39	38	30
Congress	29	28	29	34	40	40	42
Big business	29	28	20	32	33	34	26
Television	26	25	25	38	NA	NA	37

NA = Not asked.

SOURCE: Princeton Religion Research Center, Emerging Trends 6 (November, 1984).

Table 4
ATTENDANCE AT RELIGIOUS SERVICES, 1952-1980

Questions asked those acknowledging a religious preference:
1952-1968
Would you say you go to church regularly, often, seldom, or never?
1979-1980
Would you say you go to [church or synagogue] every week, almost every week, once or twice a month, a few times a year, or never?

	Regularly/ every week/ almost every week	Often/ once or twice a month	Seldom/ a few times a year	Never
1952	38%	18%	36%	8%
1956	42	18	34	6
1960	44	18	33	5
1964	45	17	31	7
1968	38	15	36	11
1972	39	12	34	15
1976	40	15	31	14
1980	40	13	32	16

SOURCE: Surveys by the Center for Political Studies of the Institute for Social Research, University of Michigan, Election Studies; latest survey 1980.

Table 5
ATTENDANCE AT RELIGIOUS SERVICES, 1958-1984

Did you, yourself, happen to attend [church or synagogue] in the last seven days?

	National	Protestant	Catholic
1958	49%	44%	74%
1961	47	43%	71%
1964	45	38	71
1967	43	39	66
1970	42	38	60
1973	40	37	55
1976	42	40	55
1978	41	40	52
1980	40	39	53
1981	41	40	53
1982	40	41	51
1983	40	39	52
1984	40	39	51

Note: Data for each year represent averages of several surveys.

SOURCE: Surveys by the Gallup Organization.

Table 6
ATTENDANCE AT RELIGIOUS SERVICES, 1972-1984

How often do you attend religious services?

	1972	1973	1974	1975	1976	1977	1978	1980	1982	1983	1984
Never	9%	14%	12%	15%	13%	14%	16%	11%	14%	14%	13%
Less than once a year	9	8	7	7	9	8	9	8	7	8	7
About once or twice a year	11	13	15	12	14	13	13	16	15	13	12
Several times a year	14	15	13	14	16	13	12	15	14	12	14
About once a month	7	6	8	7	7	7	7	7	7	7	8
2-3 times a month	9	8	9	9	7	9	10	8	8	10	8
Nearly every week	6	8	6	7	6	6	7	6	6	5	5
Every week	29	21	23	23	20	22	20	22	20	23	24
Several times a week	6	8	8	7	9	8	8	8	8	9	9

SOURCE: General Social Surveys, National Opinion Research Center, University of Chicago, February–April 1984.

Table 7
IMPORTANCE OF RELIGION

How important would you say religion is in your own life—very important, fairly important, or not very important?

	Very	Fairly	Not Very
1952	75%	20%	5%
1965	71	22	7
1978	53	33	14
1980	56	31	13
1981	55	28	16
1982	57	30	13
1983	57	30	13
1984	57	30	13

Note: The "don't know" response was 2% or less in each year and was calculated out of these figures.

SOURCE: Surveys by the Gallup Organization.

Table 8
PERCEPTIONS OF RELIGIOUS INFLUENCE ON AMERICAN LIFE

At the present time, do you think religion as a whole is increasing its influence on American life or losing its influence?

	Increasing	Same (vol.)	Losing	No Opinion
1957	69%	10%	14%	7%
1962	45	17	31	7
1967	23	14	57	6
1970	14	7	75	4
1974	31	8	56	5
1976	44	8	45	3
1978	37	10	48	5
1980	35	11	46	8
1981	38	10	46	6
1982	41	9	45	5
1984	42	14	39	6

SOURCE: Surveys by the Gallup Organization.

Table 9
IMPORTANCE OF RELIGION AND CHURCH

We would like to know how important each of these aspects of life is *for you.*
  Religion and church.

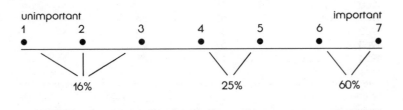

SOURCE: *General Social Surveys, National Opinion Research Center, University of Chicago, February–April 1982.*

Table 10
RELIGION AND AMERICAN POLITICS

Among a series of questions regarding attributes a president must have:

What about a candidate who . . . does not believe in God? Would you personally not vote for him for president even if you really liked him and you shared his political views? Would you say definitely not, probably not, or you might?

Definitely not	56%
Probably not	15
Maybe	27
Don't know	2

Do you agree or disagree: The real problem with Communism is that it threatens our religious and moral values.

Agree	71%
Disagree	25
Not sure/no answer	5

SOURCE: *Time/Yankelovich, Skelly, and White, 20–22 September 1983.*

Table 11
PRAYER AND PERSONAL CLOSENESS TO GOD

About how often do you pray?

	Combined 1983/1984
Several times a day	26%
Once a day	30
Several times a week	13
Once a week	8
Less than once a week	20
Never	3

How close do you feel to God most of the time?

	Combined 1983/1984
Extremely close	30%
Somewhat close	54
Not very close	10
Not close at all	5
Does not believe in God	1

SOURCE: General Social Surveys, National Opinion Research Center, University of Chicago.

Table 12
VIEWS ON THE BIBLE

Which of these statements comes closest to describing your feelings about
the Bible?

1984

a. The Bible is the actual word of God and is to be taken literally,
    word for word 38%
b. The Bible is the inspired word of God but not everything in it
    should be taken literally, word for word 48%
c. The Bible is an ancient book of fables, legends, history, and
    moral precepts recorded by men 14%

Here are four statements about the Bible, and I'd like you to tell me which
is closest to your own view.

1984

a. The Bible is God's Word and all it says is true 46%
b. The Bible was written by men inspired by God, but it contains
    some human errors 46%
c. The Bible is a good book because it was written by wise men,
    but God had nothing to do with it 1%
d. The Bible was written by men who lived so long ago that it is
    worth very little today .... *

*Less than 1%.

SOURCE: General Social Surveys, National Opinion Research Center, University of Chicago,
1984.

Table 13
PERCEPTIONS OF GOD

When you think about God, how likely are each of these images to come to your mind?

(Percentages saying extremely or somewhat likely)

	All Respondents	College-educated people, 18-29 years of age
Creator	95%	97%
Healer	91	89
Friend	88	91
Redeemer	88	89
Father	87	89
Master	80	72
Judge	77	75
Liberator	74	73
King	73	69
Lover	63	66
Mother	49	55
Spouse	34	21

SOURCE: *General Social Surveys, National Opinion Research Center, University of Chicago, combined 1983 and 1984. (In 1984, this question was only asked of one-third of the sample.)*

Table 14
OPINIONS CONCERNING LIFE AFTER DEATH

Do you believe there is a life after death?

	Yes	No	Undecided
NATIONAL	68%	24%	8%

Of course no one knows exactly what life after death would be like, but here are some ideas people have had. How likely do you feel each possibility is?

(Percentage saying very likely or somewhat likely)

	All Respondents	College-educated people, 18-29 years of age
Union with God	76%	84%
A life of peace and tranquility	74	83
Reunion with loved ones	73	82
A place of loving intellectual communion	70	80
A spiritual life, involving our mind but not our body	61	67
A paradise of pleasure and delights	52	55
A life like the one here on earth only better	47	49
A life without many things which make our present life enjoyable	38	40
A life of intense action	31	40
A pale, shadowy form of life, hardly life at all	15	12

SOURCE: *General Social Surveys, National Opinion Research Center, University of Chicago, data combined for 1983 and 1984.*

Table 15
RELIGIOUS ACTIVITY

What sort of things, if any, do you do to nourish or strengthen your faith?

Pray alone	59%
Help others	51
Attend religious services	44
Read the Bible	39
Listen to sermons or lectures	36
Meditation	32
Take walks, commune with nature	31
Receive Holy Communion	29
Watch religious TV programs	21
Read religious books other than Bible	21
Prayer in a group	19
Seek out fellow Christians	17
Pray with others for spiritual healing	14
Read religious magazines	13
Read Bible in a group	12
Evangelize, encourage others to accept Jesus	11
Spiritual counseling	8
None of the above	6

Percent saying that in the past 12 months they had:

Donated money to a charitable cause	67%
Gave money to a religious organization	60
Donated time to helping poor/disadvantaged/needy	34
Donated time to religious work	28

SOURCE: The Gallup report, "Religion In America," 1984.

Table 16
CONFIDENCE IN CHURCH OR ORGANIZED RELIGION

	Great Deal	Quite a Lot	Some	Very Little	No Opinion
National	41%	23%	22%	13%	1%
Men	38	20	24	16	2
Women	45	24	20	9	2
18-29 years	33	26	28	13	*
30-49 years	37	22	25	15	1
50 & older	52	21	14	10	3
College graduates	42	22	25	11	*
College incomplete	32	20	28	19	1
High school graduates	40	25	21	12	2
Not h.s. graduates	50	20	16	12	2
East	41	24	23	11	1
Midwest	41	20	19	19	1
South	48	20	24	6	2
West	32	30	20	16	2
Whites	39	24	22	13	2
Non-Whites	56	15	18	11	*

*Less than one percent.

SOURCE: Princeton Religion Research Center, Emerging Trends 6 (November 1984).

Table 17
ATTENDANCE AT RELIGIOUS SERVICES, 1983-1984

How often do you attend religious services?

	Never	1-2 times a year or less	Several times a year	1-3 times a month	Every/ nearly every week	Several times a week
NATIONAL	14%	20%	13%	16%	28%	9%
By Age:						
18-24 years	12	29	12	20	21	5
25-39 years	15	22	13	18	24	8
40-54 years	12	19	15	16	30	8
55-64 years	11	15	10	14	38	12
65 & older	14	16	13	11	33	13
By Education:						
Less than h.s.	17	23	11	15	24	10
H.s. grad	11	20	14	16	31	9
Some college	12	20	14	16	30	9
College grad/ post	14	18	13	19	30	7
By Age & Ed.:						
Persons 34 years and younger						
Less than h.s.	23	32	10	17	13	6
H.s. grad	12	24	15	20	23	8
College grad	12	22	12	21	27	5
35-59 years						
Less than h.s.	17	22	13	17	22	10
H.s. grad	11	19	12	15	35	9
College grad	14	16	15	17	31	8
60 years & older						
Less than h.s.	14	18	11	12	33	13
H.s. grad	12	12	13	10	41	12
College grad	16	12	12	16	30	13

SOURCE: Surveys by the National Opinion Research Center, General Social Surveys, combined 1983 and 1984.

Table 18
FREQUENCY OF PRAYER

About how often do you pray?

	Several times a day	Once a day	Several times a week	Once a week	Less than once a week	Never
NATIONAL	26%	30%	13%	8%	20%	3%
By Age:						
18-24 years	13	28	16	9	32	3
25-39 years	20	28	15	9	26	3
40-54 years	25	30	14	7	20	3
55-64 years	33	35	12	7	10	3
65 & older	46	30	8	5	9	2
By Education:						
Less than h.s.	32	29	11	7	21	2
H.s. grad	25	33	13	8	19	2
Some college	26	29	16	7	19	4
College grad/ post	20	26	15	8	25	5
By Age & Ed.:						
Persons 34 years and younger						
Less than h.s.	13	24	17	7	36	3
H.s. grad	17	29	16	11	24	3
College grad	19	27	13	7	29	5
35-59 years						
Less than h.s.	27	31	10	7	23	2
H.s. grad	27	34	13	6	18	2
College grad	21	26	16	9	23	5
60 years & older						
Less than h.s.	47	29	8	6	9	1
H.s. grad	42	33	12	5	6	1
College grad	34	25	14	7	17	5

SOURCE: Surveys by the National Opinion Research Center, General Social Surveys, combined 1983 and 1984.

Table 19
BELIEF IN LIFE AFTER DEATH

Do you believe there is a life after death?

	Yes	No
NATIONAL	76%	25%
By Age:		
18-24 years	76	24
25-39 years	79	21
40-54 years	74	26
55-64	76	24
65 & over	74	26
By Education:		
Less than h.s.	71	29
H.s. grad	79	21
Some college	79	21
College grad/post	76	24
By Age & Ed.:		
Persons 34 years and younger		
Less than h.s.	72	28
H.s. grad	77	23
College grad	84	16
35-59 years		
Less than h.s.	68	32
H.s. grad	82	18
College grad	72	28
60 years & older		
Less than h.s.	74	26
H.s. grad	79	21
College grad	66	34

SOURCE: Surveys by the National Opinion Research Center, General Social Surveys, combined 1983 and 1984.

Table 20
PERSONAL RELATIONSHIP WITH GOD

How close do you feel to God most of the time? Would you say extremely close, somewhat close, not very close, or not close at all?

	Extremely close	Somewhat close	Not very close	Not close at all	Does not believe
NATIONAL	30%	54%	8%	5%	1%
By Age:					
18-24 years	22	58	12	7	1
25-39 years	21	60	11	6	2
40-54 years	33	50	11	6	1
55-64 years	42	48	7	2	2
60 & over	44	47	6	3	1
By Education:					
Less than h.s.	39	49	8	4	1
H.s. grad	29	57	10	4	1
Some college	31	52	10	6	2
College grad/ post	20	57	12	8	3
By Age & Ed.:					
Persons 34 years and younger					
Less than h.s.	20	62	10	8	1
H.s. grad	22	61	12	5	1
College grad	19	60	9	8	3
35-59 years					
Less than h.s.	40	44	12	4	1
H.s. grad	33	53	8	5	1
College grad	22	53	14	9	3
60 years & older					
Less than h.s.	49	45	4	2	1
H.s. grad	39	51	8	2	1
College grad	28	49	12	7	3

SOURCE: Surveys by the National Opinion Research Center, General Social Surveys, combined 1983 and 1984.

Table 21
VIEWS ON THE NATURE OF THE BIBLE

Which of these statements comes closest to describing your feelings about the Bible?

The Bible is the actual word of God and is to be taken literally, word for word.

The Bible is the inspired word of God but not everything in it should be taken literally, word for word.

The Bible is an ancient book of fables, legends, history, and moral perceptions recorded by men.

	Actual Word of God	Inspired Word of God	Ancient Book of Fables
1978 National	39%	49%	12%
1981 National	41	47	12
1983 National	40	47	12
By Age:			
18-24 years	34	53	13
25-29 years	32	55	13
30-34 years	41	47	12
35-44 years	36	53	11
45-59 years	40	45	15
60 and over	53	38	9
By Education:			
Less than h.s. grad	61	33	6
H.s. grad	42	48	10
Some college/grad	21	59	19

SOURCE: Surveys by the Princeton Religion Research Center and the Gallup Organization for the Religious Coalition, 14–17 April and 28, April–1 May, 1978; and the Gallup organization, 11–14 December 1981 and 13–16 May, 1983.

Table 22
CONVERSION EXPERIENCE

Would you say that you have been "born again" or have had a "born again" experience—that is, a turning point in your life when you committed yourself to Christ?

	Yes	No
NATIONAL	34%	66%
By Age:		
18-24 years	29	71
24-29 years	25	75
30-34 years	32	68
35-44 years	45	55
45-59 years	29	71
60 and over	38	62
By Education:		
Less than h.s. grad	43	57
H.s. grad	35	65
Some college/grad	24	76

SOURCE: Survey by the Gallup Organization, 13–16 May 1983.

Table 23
PERCEPTIONS OF CHANGING AMERICAN MORAL STANDARDS

How would you describe your feelings about . . . the way moral standards have been changing in America.

	Satisfied	Dissatisfied	Don't know
NATIONAL	22%	74%	4%
By Age:			
18-24 years	36	57	7
25-29 years	34	63	3
30-34 years	27	70	3
35-44 years	17	80	3
45-59 years	18	79	2
60 and over	10	85	5
By Education:			
Less than h.s. grad	17	77	6
H.s. grad	21	75	4
Some college/grad	27	70	2

Note: Satisfied = extremely satisfied and fairly satisfied
      Dissatisfied = somewhat dissatisfied and very dissatisfied

SOURCE: Survey by the Gallup Organization, 13–16 May 1983.

Table 24
PERCEPTIONS OF THE AMERICAN RELIGIOUS CLIMATE

How would you describe your feelings about . . . the religious or spiritual climate in America?

	Satisfied	Dissatisfied	Don't know
NATIONAL	40%	51%	9%
By Age:			
18-24 years	49	43	8
25-29 years	49	46	5
30-34 years	37	56	7
35-44 years	35	62	3
45-59 years	41	50	9
60 and over	34	52	14
By Education:			
Less than h.s. grad	38	49	14
H.s. grad	42	51	7
Some college/grad	40	54	6

Note: Satisfied = extremely satisfied and fairly satisfied
Dissatisfied = somewhat dissatisfied and very dissatisfied

SOURCE: Survey by the Gallup Organization, 13–16 May 1983.

Table 25
CONNECTICUT MUTUAL SURVEYS OF THE
BELIEFS AND VALUES OF THE ELITE COMPARED TO THE GENERAL PUBLIC

Do you consider yourself a religious person?

	Yes	No
General public	74%	26%
Leaders	66	34
Religion	100	0
Business	80	20
Military	67	33
Voluntary associations	64	36
News media	64	36
Education	63	37
Government	57	43
Law and justice	53	47
Science	50	50

How frequently do you attend religious services?

	Frequently	Occasionally	Never
General public	44%	38%	18%
Leaders	43	36	21
Religion	96	4	0
Military	48	38	14
Business	47	42	11
Voluntary associations	38	42	20
Education	36	41	23
Law and justice	34	42	24
News media	33	40	27
Science	31	36	33
Government	28	47	25

How frequently do you engage in prayer?

	Frequently	Occasionally	Never
General public	57%	32%	11%
Leaders	48	32	20
Religion	95	4	1
Business	67	25	8
Voluntary associations	46	32	22
Military	44	40	16
News media	44	32	24
Education	40	33	27
Government	38	41	21
Law and justice	33	41	26
Science	27	40	33

How frequently do you feel that God loves you?

	Frequently	Occasionally	Never
General public	73%	21%	6%
Leaders	54	23	23
Religion	96	2	2
Business	70	18	12
News media	53	29	18
Voluntary associations	53	20	27
Military	50	33	17
Government	48	26	26
Law and justice	44	27	29
Education	40	28	32
Science	31	31	38

Was there a specific time in your adult life when you made a personal commitment to Christ that changed your life?

	Yes	No
General public	47%	53%
Leaders	33	67
Religion	74	26
Business	37	63
Voluntary associations	35	65
News media	29	71
Military	25	75
Government	22	78
Law and justice	21	79
Education	20	80
Science	18	82

SOURCE: Survey by Research and Forecasts for Connecticut Mutual Life Insurance, 1 September–15 November 1980.

Table 26
PUBLIC OPINION ON SCHOOL PRAYER

What are views on the reading of the Lord's Prayer or Bible verses in public schools? Do you think it should be *required* in all public schools, *not allowed* in any public schools, or that it should be up to each state or local community to decide?

Required	32%
Not Allowed	9%
Communities Decide	60%

SOURCE: Survey by the National Opinion Research Center, General Social Surveys, 1974.

Do you favor or oppose an amendment to the Constitution that would permit organized prayers in public schools?

	Favor	Oppose	Not Sure
May 1982	68%	27%	5%
August 1982	65	29	6

SOURCE: Surveys by NBC News/Associated Press.

Would you favor or oppose an amendment to the Constitution that would permit organized prayers to be said in the public schools?

Favor	66%
Oppose	29
No opinion	5

SOURCE: Survey by CBS News/New York Times, 13–18 September 1982.

Question asked regarding the 2 November 1982 election: Suppose you could vote on key issues as well as candidates. Please tell me how you would vote on the following proposition.

I favor a constitutional amendment
to permit prayer in the public schools.   73%
I oppose a constitutional amendment
to permit prayers in the public schools.   27%

SOURCE: Survey by the Gallup Organization, 17–20 September 1982.

The United States Supreme Court has ruled that no state or local government may *require* the reading of the Lord's Prayer or Bible verses in public schools. What are your views on this—do you approve or disapprove of the court ruling?

	Approve	Disapprove
1974	32%	68%
1975	36	64
1977	34	66
1982	39	61
1983	41	59

SOURCE: Surveys by the National Opinion Research Center, General Social Surveys.

Do you favor or oppose allowing voluntary prayer in schools?

	Registered voters
Favor allowing voluntary prayer	79%
Oppose	15
Don't know	5

Note: Sample size = 1,025 registered voters.

SOURCE: Survey by Penn & Schoen Associates for the Garth Analysis, 24–28 June 1983.

Do you approve or disapprove of a constitutional amendment to permit voluntary prayers in public schools, or haven't you heard enough about that yet to say?

Approve	74%
Disapprove	20%
Haven't heard enough to say	3%
Not sure	3%

SOURCE: Survey by the Los Angeles Times, 26–30 June 1983.

Do you favor or oppose allowing prayer in schools?

	Registered Voters
Favor	67%
Oppose	22
Don't know	11

Note: Sample size = 1,016 registered voters.

SOURCE: Survey by Time/Yankelovich, Skelly, and White, 20–22 September 1983.

Do you favor or oppose a constitutional amendment to allow daily prayers to be recited in school classrooms?

	Favor	Oppose	Not Sure
February 1982 national	69%	28%	3%
April 1984 likely voters	67	29	4

Note: Sample size for February 1982 = 1,253 adults; for April 1984 = 1,270 likely voters.

SOURCE: Surveys by Louis Harris and Associates, latest that of 4–8 April 1984.

Generally speaking, do you approve or disapprove of prayers in public schools?

	Registered Voters
Approve	77%
Disapprove	19
Not sure	4

SOURCE: Survey by the Los Angeles Times, 28 April–3 May 1984.

Table 27
RELIGIOUS INFLUENCES IN THE 1984 PRESIDENTIAL ELECTION

Did your clergyman encourage you to vote for either Reagan or Mondale?

	All Voters		Reagan Voters		Mondale Voters	
	Yes for Reagan	Yes for Mondale	Yes for R	Yes for M	Yes for R	Yes for M
Nationally	4%	4%	6%	1%	2%	8%
In the East	3	4	4	1	2	8
South	4	5	5	1	2	12
Midwest	5	3	6	1	2	7
West	5	3	7	1	1	6
In West Virginia	5	5	7	2	3	9
North Carolina	5	7	8	2	1	15
Alabama	6	11	9	2	1	29
Texas	5	7	6	1	2	18
Mississippi	7	10	10	1	2	24
In New Hampshire	3	1	3	1	2	3
Vermont	4	4	5	2	2	5
Massachusetts	4	3	5	1	2	5
In Pennsylvania	5	4	5	1	6	8
New Jersey	5	4	6	2	3	8
New York	5	5	8	2	1	8
In Michigan	5	5	5	2	3	11
Iowa	5	3	7	2	3	4
Illinois	5	4	7	1	2	9
Ohio	5	5	7	2	1	9
Minnesota	4	3	4	2	3	5
In Oregon	4	5	7	3	1	8
California	4	4	6	1	1	8

SOURCE: Election Day polls taken by CBS News, 6 November 1984.

Table 28
RELIGIOUS MAKE-UP AND VOTING PATTERNS
OF THE 1984 PRESIDENTIAL ELECTORATE

	Reagan	Mondale
Mormons (2% of electorate)	85%	15%
Presbyterians (7%)	68	32
Lutherans (7%)	66	34
Methodists (13%)	65	35
All Protestants (62%)	61	39
Episcopalians (3%)	60	40
Roman Catholics (28%)	59	41
ALL VOTERS	59	41
Baptists (22%)	51	49
Atheists (1%)	34	66
Jews (3%)	32	68

* * *

Voters who reported having had "a born-again experience—a turning point . . . when you committed yourself to Jesus Christ" (39%)	63	37
Voters who said they had not had a born-again experience (61%)	57	43

SOURCE: *Election Day survey, Los Angeles* Times, *6 November 1984.*

Table 29
VIEWS ON THE VALIDITY OF REASONS FOR LEGAL ABORTION

	Threat to mother's health	Pregnancy caused by rape	Threat of defect in baby	Can't afford more children	Single/ does not want to marry	Married/ does not want more children	Wants abortion for any reason
ALL RESPONDENTS	86%	82%	80%	45%	42%	41%	36%
By Age & Education:							
Persons 34 years and younger							
Less than h.s.	89	76	76	36	30	31	25
H.s. grad	91	84	83	46	40	40	36
College grad	94	89	85	63	63	60	56
35-59 years							
Less than h.s.	86	62	71	35	30	30	24
H.s. grad	89	80	79	42	41	40	35
College grad	93	84	83	61	60	60	56
60 years & older							
Less than h.s.	85	79	70	33	28	25	20
H.s. grad	89	85	82	42	40	39	35
College grad	93	91	90	57	56	48	52
By Political Ideology:							
Liberal	92	86	83	57	54	54	48
Moderate	91	83	83	45	42	41	37
Conservative	87	76	75	40	38	36	32
By Race:							
White	91	83	81	46	43	42	37
Black	83	72	69	38	30	34	29
By Religion:							
Protestant	90	81	79	42	39	38	33
Catholic	86	78	76	39	36	35	31
Jewish	99	99	97	91	88	83	76
None	95	91	92	71	68	70	63
By Frequency of Church Attendance:							
Never	94	91	88	65	62	61	55
1-2 times a year or less	95	90	89	58	54	54	48
Several times a year	96	89	89	55	49	48	40
1-3 times a month	91	84	82	46	42	42	36
Every/nearly every week	85	75	71	31	30	28	26
Several times a week	73	54	53	14	11	11	11

SOURCE: General Social Survey, National Opinion Research Center, University of Chicago, combined 1983 and 1984.

Table 30
GENERAL OPINIONS CONCERNING ABORTION

Do you favor or oppose an amendment to the Constitution which would give Congress the authority to prohibit abortions?

Favor	19%
Oppose	75
Not sure	6

SOURCE: Survey by NBC News/Associated Press, 18–19 January 1982.

Do you personally believe that abortion is wrong? If yes, do you think abortion should be illegal?

Abortion is not wrong	44%
Abortion is wrong but should not be illegal	22
Abortion is wrong and should be illegal	27
Not sure	7

SOURCE: Survey by NBC News/Associated Press, 27–28 January 1982.

Do you agree or disagree with the following statement: "The decision to have an abortion should be left to the woman and her physician."

	Agree	Disagree	Not sure
January 1982	77%	20%	3%
August 1982	77	20	3

SOURCE: Surveys by NBC News/Associated Press.

There is a proposal for a Constitutional amendment which would give individual states the right to outlaw abortions statewide. Do you favor or oppose such an amendment?

	Registered Voters
Favor	47%
Oppose	46
No Opinion	7

Note: Registered voters = 70% of sample.

SOURCE: Survey by CBS News/New York Times, 13–18 September 1982.

Question asked regarding the 2 November 1982 election: Suppose you could vote on key issues as well as candidates. Please tell me how you would vote on the following propositions:

I favor a ban on federal financing of abortions.	44%
I oppose a ban on federal financing of abortions.	56%

SOURCE: Survey by the Gallup Organization, 17–20 September 1982.

Do you think abortions should be legal under any circumstances, legal under only certain circumstances, or illegal in all circumstances?

Legal (all)	23%
Legal (certain)	58
Illegal (all)	16
No Opinion	3

SOURCE: Survey by the Gallup Organization, 24–27 June 1983.

Do you favor or oppose a law eliminating all federal funds for abortions for poor women?

	Registered voters
Favor	35%
Oppose	58
Don't Know	6

Note: Sample size = 1,010 registered voters.

SOURCE: Survey by Penn & Schoen Associates for the Garth Analysis, 26–30 August 1983.

Do you favor or oppose a constitutional amendment to prohibit almost all abortions?

	Registered voters
Favor	36%
Oppose	57
Don't Know	7

Note: Sample size = 1,010 registered voters.

SOURCE: Survey by Penn & Schoen Associates for the Garth Analysis, 26–30 August 1983.

Should abortion be permitted under all circumstances, under some circumstances, or under no circumstances?

	Registered voters
Under all circumstances	21%
Under some circumstances	67
Under no circumstances	10
Don't know	2

Note: Sample size = 1,010 registered voters.

SOURCE: Survey by Penn & Schoen Associates for the Garth Analysis, 30 August 1983.

Do you favor or oppose . . . a constitutional amendment to ban [legalized] abortion?

	Favor	Oppose	Not sure
February 1982 national	33%	61%	6%
July 1982 national	31	62	7
April 1984 likely voters	34	59	7

Note: Sample sizes for February 1982 = 1,253 adults; for July 1982 = 1,250 adults; for April 1984 = 1,270 likely voters.

SOURCE: Surveys by Louis Harris and Associates.

Do you approve of a constitutional amendment to prohibit abortion?

Approve	23%
Disapprove	77%

Note: Sample size = 7,310 voters as they left booths.

SOURCE: Survey by the Los Angeles Times, 6 November 1984.

Should abortion be legal?

Yes, as it is now	42%
Only in extreme circumstances	29%
No	25%
No Opinion	4%

Note: Sample size = 8,671 voters as they left booths. The survey was not conducted in Washington, Hawaii, or Alaska.

SOURCE: Survey by CBS News/New York Times, 6 November 1984.

Participants

Brian Benestad
Department of Theology
and Religious Studies
University of Scranton

Peter L. Berger
University Professors Program
Boston University

Theodore Caplow
Department of Sociology
University of Virginia

Allan Carlson
The Rockford Institute

Midge Decter
Committee for the Free World

Edward Dobson
Fundamentalist Journal

Ernest Fortin
Department of Theology
Boston College

George Gallup, Jr.
Gallup Organization, Inc.
Princeton, New Jersey

Os Guiness
Theologian and Author
Oxford, England

Ed Hindson
School of Religion
Liberty University

Paul Johnson
Historian and author
Buckinghamshire, England

Dean M. Kelley
Division of Church and Society
National Council of Churches

Lyman A. Kellstedt
Department of Political Science
Wheaton College

Everett Ladd
The Roper Center
University of Connecticut

George M. Marsden
Department of History
Calvin College

Jay Mechling
American Studies Program
University of California at Davis

Richard John Neuhaus
The Rockford Institute Center
on Religion & Society

Mark Noll
Department of History
Wheaton College

Michael Novak
American Enterprise Institute

Daniel J. O'Neil
Department of Political Science
University of Arizona

Ralph Potter
Divinity School
Harvard University

Diane Ravitch
Teacher's College
Columbia University

Stanley Rothman
Department of Government
Smith College

Paul T. Stallsworth
The Rockford Institute Center
   on Religion & Society

Steven Tipton
Candler School of Theology
Emory University

Robert Woodson
National Center for
   Neighborhood
   Enterprise

Robert Wuthnow
Department of Sociology
Princeton University